FEMININE SPIRITUALITY

FEMININE SPIRITUALITY

Reflections on the Mysteries of the Rosary

by

Rosemary Haughton

PAULIST PRESS
New York/Ramsey, N.J./Toronto

Library of Congress
Catalog Card Number: 76-24438

ISBN: 0-8091-1982-X

Published by Paulist Press
Editorial Office: 1865 Broadway, N.Y., N.Y. 10023
Business Office: 545 Island Road, Ramsey, N.J. 07446

Printed and bound in the
United States of America

Contents

HOW THIS BOOK WAS WRITTEN

It all began with the pump. Where we live, we had not yet finished building our house, so we lived in trailers, and the water came from a well. At first we hauled it up in buckets but later on we found an old hand pump, on a tip, and brought it home. We fixed it up, and after that we pumped the water through a hose pipe to tanks in the trailers. One day we'll have a wind pump, but meanwhile everyone has to do some hand pumping each day.

It's not hard work but at first I found it extremely boring, standing there pushing and pulling, counting the strokes to make myself pump a reasonable amount before I thankfully left it to the next person.

Then one day the rhythmic movement of pumping somehow linked itself in my mind with another kind of rhythm, that of prayer—rosary prayer. I am not sure why I made the connection, the two things simply jumped together in my mind. Instead of counting, I realized that I could time my turn at the pump with prayers, and do two useful things at one time. I discovered that one "Hail Mary" was twelve strokes long, and five decades plus the other prayers accounted for quite a lot of water going into the tanks.

So day by day I stood at the pump with a rosary in one hand and the pump handle in the other. Soon I found that all kinds of ideas were flowing with the water, ideas that welled up from the deep springs within myself, drawn by the power of the words and the fifteen "mysteries," which are so familiar and yet so peculiar.

All this happened at a time when I, like so many other women, was wrestling with the questions about who, and what, a woman is. In what ways are we different from men? Are the differences fundamental or learned? What is a woman's role—spiritually as well as economically and domestically? Is there a feminine aspect of spirit and growth, for men and women?

The ideas that flowed through my mind while I pumped and prayed came gently, yet clear, strong, and as refreshing as the water. They are the basis of this book. I have worked on them as I have written them down, but the essence of them is the understanding I gained when I was trying to pray, not to write.

The one thing I discovered, which seems to me especially important, is that I was not considering simply fifteen isolated incidents or aspects of the life of Christ and his Mother. I was watching the unfolding of a continuous action, each "scene" essentially but deeply and unexpectedly linked to the next and with the rest, and that this unfolding had to do not only with what actually happened on earth to Jesus and Mary, but what is *always* happening when God's Word is spoken in human flesh.

This is, then, a reflection on the rosary from a

special point of view. The things that the fifteen mysteries "contain" are endless and flow out to many different concerns and situations and mentalities. The concern here is a woman's concern, at a time when many women are trying to discover the fullness and uniqueness of the humanity that is feminine, and of the feminine *in* humanity—men and women. It's very simple, not a theological analysis but an attempt to communicate a common experience. It presupposes, perhaps, a certain sympathy.

I

A Woman Says "Yes"

It begins with an assent. A woman says "yes" to something that is going to change her whole life and the lives of others. She does not know exactly how or even precisely why. It is all deep down, barely touching consciousness, yet the assent has to be real and full or it doesn't work. A new principle of life is implanted; the new life begins its unfolding, yet it is hidden; as far as appearances go nothing has happened. Mary's assent, the assent of any woman who has conceived, is the beginning.

This also happens with knowing God. Perhaps religion has always been some kind of a reasonably acceptable routine, a good way to live, a firm but not very exciting context for living. Or maybe it has never been known. I come across it anew, in a friend, a place, an experience. Either way, there has to be a point at which one says "yes" to something new, strange, fundamental. It can be very quiet. It probably was quiet with Mary. It can be so quiet that after a time it is possible to wonder if it really happened. Nothing has changed, I'm still the same person. I find it difficult, if not impossible, to explain. (Mary couldn't explain it, not even to her husband.) Yet there has been this assent, quite definite, committing me to—I'm not sure what, but it is greater than I; it is not within my control, yet is myself; deep down it is *I* who live by this new life.

How does this assent happen? It doesn't happen to everyone. We can resist and prevent it, and never even notice—because until we let ourselves become aware of the invitation, we can't respond to it. And we don't want to listen, because it means giving up control over our lives.

This is something that many women are afraid to do. They have become conscious of themselves as people, whole people who are not dependent on male approval. They want to make their own decisions, steer their own ship where they see fit. They are afraid of attempts to make them dependent, to attach them to people or work, for this limits their freedom. This need to pull free, to have a sense of independent value, is similar to the need adolescents have to discover their own selves in separation from their families. But it is far more difficult because these women are adults, already formed, and trying hard to know what, in that formation, is their very own and what is keeping them confined in a "feminine image" created according to a masculine myth.

It is no wonder the invitation to surrender to faith seems like spiritual suicide to some women. It only seems so, however. The hard-won separateness is not achieved for its own sake, but so that a human being may be able *freely* to give herself to love. It is only by being herself that a woman can truly give—the fearful, insecure individual is imprisoned within her own defenses; she cannot give; she can only cling and demand.

Then, too, personal independence is not a thing to achieve and then keep. It is part of a process, like a growing plant. To try to stop the process does not stop the person from growing, rather the growth goes wrong, it becomes grotesque and bitter. Such a person needs constantly to prove independence by rejecting others, pushing away experiences that threaten, refusing closeness or commitment. Some women are like that; they are afraid to listen, to become aware of the invitation to love because love means I am no longer my own—and yet, only through it do I truly discover myself.

One of the things that makes it difficult for a woman to listen to this strange invitation is that we have been taught to assume that, for a woman, the invitation she hears is bound to be embodied in a man, and that if she says "yes" she will henceforward be his possession. It can be a husband or a "masculine" Church that assumes the right to possess and direct her.

Human beings are not each other's possession; the lover's language of passionate possession is misleading. The sense of self-discovery in another, in sexual love (which makes people use words such as "possessing" about the experience) really needs to be viewed from the other angle. What is happening is not that one person possesses the other, but that the one is prepared to "give and hazard all he hath" to the other and *therefore* to make the sense of self available to the beloved. This should be the way it is in listening to God in a Christian community context.

To listen to the invitation, in whatever way it comes—as human love, as the demands of a form of service (to people or to art or learning) or as a call of faith—is to open oneself, to become aware of the possibility of a new life, a radically "other" life, yet intimately mine. To assent to it is to begin a new era; after that anything can happen, which is why that "yes" is so impractical and yet is the absolute, unalterable, essential beginning of wholeness and truth.

When a woman says "yes" to the invitation that is spoken to her, by whatever messenger (and God's angels come at times in odd clothes) then, once more, the Word is made flesh.

Mary conceived the child whom we recognize as Savior and Lord. We know from our whole religious tradition that something of revolutionary importance and on a cosmic scale happened when Mary said "yes" to God's messenger. We can never know how she felt, but she certainly didn't have our two-thousand-years-after view of the event. First of all, it happened to her, to her personal, inmost self, as it happens to every mother. The moment at which a woman accepts the fact that she has conceived has a quality of both terror and joy, yet under these, deep within her heart, is a little pool of certainty which somehow assures her even when tempests of conflicting feelings blow over it. The fact of assent creates that core of certainty, of peace. This womanly experience is not merely an image of what happens when a person accepts the invitation to let love in, it is also an example of it. To assent to actual physical conception is one way of letting the Word become flesh. The Spirit in man has once more been welcomed in his working and growing in humankind and anything can happen. There are many other ways in which a woman or a man can give assent to the invitation to let love in, but this is one way. It is an experience which a woman—even if she never conceives—can reflect on from "inside," and appreciate in a special way.

There is a sense of panic that often follows the realization that a baby has been conceived, even when the child is wanted and longed for, perhaps even more so in such cases, for the struggle to come to terms with and accept an *un*wanted pregnancy signifies that when the assent is finally made, some of the panic has already been overcome. This panic arises from a feeling of being trapped. The process has begun; this child is going to grow; one day it will be born and there is nothing one can do about it. From now on my life will be ruled by this knowledge; I'm no longer free, no longer my own person. Even for women who have no fear of childbirth, there often is present this sense of unreasonable recoil, like a wild animal suddenly realizing that it is in a cage.

The panic passes because the courage implicit in the assent to the child has reason as its ally, and the two plus the spiritual toughness that most women have and men find so hard to understand, reduce the panic to its proper place.

One scripture scholar has suggested that the famous passage in Isaiah where the prophet proclaims that "a virgin (that is, a young girl) shall conceive and bear a son" is not so much a prophecy of Mary's virginity, as an assertion that God's covenant cannot fail; just as certainly as the conception of a child is followed by its birth, so God's promise is followed by its fulfillment. Nothing is more certain than this sequence, says the prophet, and the child is "God with us." Here is both the sense of inevitability and the assurance that what has to be faced is life, and is glorious.

Yet the fear is a valid feeling, a true indication of part of the nature of the change that is taking place. When I assent to God, I "give and hazard all I have," I am no longer my own person, yet I begin to discover myself. The beginning of this discovery is in that little, deep pool of peace of which we become conscious from time to time. In moments of quiet, even in the middle of bustle and noise, a woman can be aware of this, and know that the life which is beginning in her and of her is not hers alone. The deep, clear pool which she knows is linked to the flowing of great underground streams of the water of life. Somewhere in that water the "self" is living and growing. It is not hers to command, rather it shapes her and pushes her and makes demands on her. A kind of freedom has gone, but the knowledge of a deeper and radical freedom is beginning to replace it. It can grow, if that assent to the Word of love is lived out. There is a long struggle ahead, already dimly felt, yet it is common for women in early pregnancy to feel (even if they are physically uncomfortable and mentally worried) a curious commitment to the present moment. There is a gathering of herself together to cope with things *now*, and the feeling that later on can take care of itself.

This is what such assent does, for it is an act of love and commitment to a process, and the thing is not mine to order, so all I can do is cherish the newly discovered love and cope with whatever comes along, bit by little bit. It is very private, this feeling, a sort of enclosing hermitage of clear but inarticulate knowing. There is not necessarily any joy, there may be too much worry, or work, or physical stress for that. There is only the sense of entering on something that matters, the wrench of surrender, the confidence that it is worthwhile, the courage (a rather dogged, even quietly humorous kind of courage) to keep working as usual.

All this applies to the woman who has conceived and assented to it. It can be applied to Mary, who did not, after all, have an easy time of it. It is true of all those, men and women, who bring themselves, struggling, doubtful, half-wondering if they are wrong after all, to give themselves to a purpose which is not their own, yet is, in another sense, most intimately their own. Each time the eternal Word takes flesh.

This happens, most obviously, in one great transforming moment, as it did for Mary, or in a great mystical or conversion experience though the consequences are slow to reveal themselves. It happens in many little moments, when God sends messengers into our lives, and their invitation is accepted or rejected. It happens to a person needing comfort or help, perhaps an irritating person, at a busy moment. Or something beautiful—a flower struggling to grow among city concrete, or a sunset, the turn of a child's head, a snatch of music, or laughter—something which demands a response to the glory of the Spirit in the world, only we often prefer not to see it for it disturbs our comfortable cynicism and selfishness. Or perhaps some humiliation comes, we feel neglected, tied to a dull, thankless job, or we lose a friend, or an opportunity, and again the invitation is to let the experience in, let it work and grow. Whatever it is, it asks that we do not snatch and hug the experience to ourselves but let it take us over, changing us, making us living and helping us to grow.

Apparently trivial moments, even tinier than these, or profound, once-for-all conversions—all have the same character. An invitation is heard and attended to and accepted. Thereafter we are not our own, nor on our own. We are given and anything can happen.

II
Blessed Is She Who Believed

A new life is growing, the experience of God once implanted does not wait for permission. It grows, and changes, and makes itself felt. Whereas at first it draws in, creating awareness of a stillness at the heart of experience, this is only fleeting, no more than a pause, a breathing, a realization. It can't remain an interior, private thing. It has to communicate, it *demands* communication.

When the Word of life was conceived in Mary she went to share the knowledge as soon as she could. But not with just anyone, not even, at that stage, with her husband. That was for later. At first, the need was to tell the news to someone who shared the experience in some measure. The thing to be shared was not merely the fact of a baby coming, but the coming of God into one's life in a wholly new way. The person with whom she can share such knowledge, so soon, has to be someone whose life also has been invaded by God, whose future has been changed and taken over. The results reach beyond imagining, even beyond praying, but both know that they are involved in a huge movement of spiritual energy. Both are, in their own way "blessed among women" for God is "with us" through them.

His blessing is extended to each human being who assents to his invitation, and to each, in her turn, comes this profound need to *say aloud* the truth which so far has been only a wordless, lived knowledge. Any woman who has brought herself (perhaps with shuddering and struggle) to take on willingly the task (or person, calling, suffering) that is before her knows the craving, so violent it aches, for someone to tell, someone who knows what it's like, who is "older" in some sense, yet on a level by this shared experience.

Sometimes there is no one to tell. The craving can be a gnawing continual pain, never healed, something one must learn to live with. To escape it in part by confiding in an unsuitable person, simply for the relief of expressing the experience, can have bad results, because the other person doesn't really understand, even if he or she tries to do so.

Imagine what might have happened if Mary had confided in a village friend, a nice, comforting, motherly person. If there had been no one else, she might have been driven to that, hoping in the other woman's habitual kindness and experience. In all probability, her story would have been disbelieved. At best, it would have been regarded as a pious girl's fantasy to be kindly discouraged. Or, if the truth of the pregnancy were proved, the story would be seen as a pathetic attempt to cover up a guilty conscience. A kindly woman might be willing to conceal the "truth," shelter and sympathize, but the significance of the happening could not be communicated. The new life in Mary could only be damaged.

It happens so easily. The person who has responded to God is very vulnerable at first, uncertain, eager, needing support and reassurance. The vast weight of uncomprehending, kindly common sense can even shatter the budding confidence, persuade the newly awakening spirit that the whole experience is a delusion, a distraction from the real business of life, an hysterical episode to be "got over" by rest and common sense and a new dress.

An even worse kind of confidante—and an even more superficially attractive one—is the pious enthusiast. There are plenty about. Such people are always searching for "spiritual experiences" with the accent on the experience. They are expert at detecting atmospheres—of holiness or of evil—and are full of stories of the thrill they felt at such a place, or during such a Scripture reading, or on encountering so-and-so. They are perfectly sincere people, genuinely thirsty for the reality behind appearances, but they are like gourmets, who can't simply enjoy the deliciousness of good food, but make a cult of flavor, demanding (and endlessly recounting) taste sensations as reassurance that life is worth living. They cannot, like most people, eat dull meals when necessary, or appreciate the pleasantness of ordinary food lovingly and skillfully cooked. For them, such a diet makes life meaningless, even repulsive. So too for the pietist.

That is why they love to be confidantes. If "spiritual experiences" of their own are not as abundant as they might be, they welcome the experiences of others, and they especially like the feeling of being "in the know," the one trusted repository of a great secret. Then, too, the sense of being so extremely humble as to appreciate selflessly the superior experience of another has a special flavor.

Such a confidante, however sincere and even genuinely good, can be a disaster for the woman driven by the glorious and yet painful desire to share "the wonderful works of God." She is a disaster because she is uniquely interested in the *feelings* involved, and in the status the event gives to the blessed one (and to herself). She may give to the confidante a much needed sense of importance and reassurance, but this attitude saps the truth of the event. The tentative, open heart is confused and disturbed because praise and appreciation are being given, not to the One who blesses but to the blessed who did nothing but assent. The singleness of heart which made the assent possible is divided and muddled with wondering how one should "live up to" the new life, display it, portray it.

Yet all that is really needed is the chance to see, reflected in another's mind, the peace and the still fearful love that belong to the knowledge of new life. Very little needs to be said, for both know, yet *something* must be said. The thing that has happened needs words, and the person who can help to discover the right words is one for whom those words have a similar significance.

It was not when the message came to her that Mary found words to express what had happened, but, as Luke tells it, only when she and her cousin met and knew the truth in each other. The account rings true. This is how it is. The words Luke uses are carefully composed with overtones from the Jewish Scripture, especially from the thanksgiving song of Hannah when she found she had conceived a son by God's blessing, but they are (for that reason) a true expression of this welling up of triumph and praise—sheer glory pouring itself out in whatever words can best convey such things.

The newly conceived Word requires words, the happening doesn't, in a sense, fully happen until some way is found to make the fact known outwardly as well as inwardly. We all know how the effort of explaining a thing to another person clarifies it for oneself, even revealing unexpected implications. But when the thing one knows is still scarcely grasped and yet of overwhelming importance, then the words to tell it, to make it "happen" in an essential new dimension, are hard to find. This is why people sometimes find that poetry, or some other words from a mind especially gifted, can best express what is so deeply, newly, personal. And when the words come—halting or fluent—something happens to the whole experience. By being put into words and shared it becomes possible to "take hold of it" in a new way. This is very important. Even in ordinary physical childbirth, the way the fact is understood makes or mars the whole relationship, as advocates of natural childbirth emphasize.

When people undergo a great spiritual experience (or even a little one) and can't find a person to share with, or words to say it, it very quickly fades. They can't take hold of it, grasp what it means in terms of *doing*. We need to *do* something about such comings of God, great and small. To do nothing is to be left, eventually, with nothing but a faint and worrying nostalgia for a lost moment. To find words is to know the meaning of the event, at least tentatively, and so to have some idea of what consequences follow. To find words is not an "extra," it is essential to the proper unfolding and growth of the happening. This Mary knew, and all women know, though sometimes they are denied the chance to make it true. Some even resort to diaries, confiding to a second self that which has to be said. Somehow, words must be found.

They must, too, be the right words. As suggested, the wrong confidante, who uses and encourages words that distort the true meaning, can harm or even destroy what has happened. This is why there is such a thing as "religious language." It can become a mere formality like poetry learned in school in order to pass examinations. But, like poetry, the language of worship is created to be a way of saying the happenings of God. It is not everyday language; it is special and it uses words that have collected echoes as they passed through the centuries, so that to use them is to say more than the dictionary meaning. Like an incantation, they conjure up a "cloud of witnesses" to share in announcing the coming of God into his world yet again and since forever.

Ordinary, everyday words sometimes can help to "cleanse" older ones, if we have allowed these to become merely a fog of antiquated syllables. There are times when this fog happens, and people find it hard to use the older words meaningfully. Then, more "everyday" speech helps to clear the fog. But that is all it can do, which is why many people are faintly puzzled by the unsatisfying quality of some of the newer liturgy. These things can't be hurried, the echoes need time, use, the polishing of years of loving use, before they can shimmer with layer upon layer of meaning.

That is why, when Mary came to Elizabeth, she celebrated her motherhood in words crowded with echoes of her people's strange history. And this is why, when the right confidante is hard to find, and the need of one is profound, the happening that craves words to discover itself can find form and meaning principally in old, familiar words. People struggling to know what God is doing in them remember that woman who knew God's action in its most profound manner. So, with a sense of extraordinary release, discovery, companionship, we find ourselves saying: Hail, Mary—full of grace, the Lord is with thee—and with me, in my way, and so, blessed are we among women. Pray for me now, because now I'm beginning to know what you know. Help me to know it more fully, to bring it to birth.

III
Mary Treasured These Things

It has to come to birth. The first sharing, the finding of words, are a foretelling; it is not complete, it is just a way to realize that there has to be a birth.

Before a baby is born parents discuss its sex, its name, even its possible career. Yet all this doesn't seem quite real. It kicks and bumps around as it grows, its presence is undeniable, even some character traits can be guessed at by its behavior. Yet the discussions are really only fantasy. The bond between mother and unborn child is deep but not yet fully personal.

"Pen pals" can be interesting and a real relationship can grow, but to meet the person one wrote to begins quite a different relationship. A friendship maintained over years by letter may be full and intimate yet quite misleading when a reunion occurs.

There is a profound and essential difference between knowing with the mind only, and knowing a person. Humankind could have been taught all the spiritual wisdom of saints and sages by word of mouth and in books, and it could never have added up to the knowledge of God which is Jesus, a person, a man—a baby.

Knowing a person happens on many levels. Knowing *about* that person is important. If I know, for instance, that he/she has had an unhappy childhood, or has suffered a bereavement, that helps me to understand better certain reactions, expressions, perhaps certain failures. If I can interpret behavior and feelings more accurately, I am able to come closer, to know better. But to know *about* is no substitute for the knowing which can never be fully expressed in words. The Word of God was made flesh, not books. The books are useful, they help us to understand what happened, what happens. But there had to be a birth. The Word became not just flesh, a generalized humanness, but a person, a particular little boy, with ears set just so, weighing so much, perhaps inheriting his mother's eyes.

A person is a self, a separate, potentially whole being. Once a child is born, he or she is recognizable as personal, and the relationship between mother and child becomes one between two persons. Before birth it is private, unassailable, hers, even if she has given herself to a process she cannot control or direct. (Only destroy. Death can be dealt by humankind, life cannot.)

But once the child has come from the womb he or she is no longer private. There is not one relationship, but several, and potentially thousands. This is a public event. To that extent, the mother who has just borne a child has begun to lose it. Just as she could not order her conception, but only assent to it, so she cannot alter the inevitable passage away from her. It is part of the process, it is what she assented to, even if she didn't know it.

There is an anguish of birth that has nothing to do with labor pain (which is not essential, either physically or spiritually). The anguish has to do with the realization that the newly born is now, and will be increasingly, vulnerable to harm of all kinds. It is simply a fact about life, about physical life and spiritual life.

The newly discovered consciousness of glory cannot remain in the womb forever, any more than a baby can. A time of quiet interior growth there is, shared only with the few who can fully understand, but the way it grows means that a time comes (it may be weeks, or years, even decades) when it has to be born, to become public, to begin to be lost to the one who knew it and bore it. That is how things are, that is how it happens. It is part of the price that has to be paid.

Women appreciate this more readily than men, because they have the capacity for realizing it bodily, even if they don't in practice ever bear a child. There is a capacity for a sort of unsentimental acceptance of loss in most women which men find hard to understand, and often interpret as proof that women are less sensitive. Little boys are often much more overthrown by the death of a bird, or a beloved relative, because they lack the feminine grasp of the inevitability of losing what one loves.

To love a person is, in some sense, to give birth to him/her. Real love means an assent to the incoming of the spirit, a new thing has been accepted and has to be nurtured, but also it must be freed, allowed to take its independent way, and so be lost to some extent. The realization that this losing is an unavoidable part of loving is something that even little girls seem to come to terms with. It can make them seem hard.

It can make them truly hard, if they refuse to accept the loss into themselves. It is as if the child, once born, were disowned for fear of the pain of loving what one cannot possess. Perhaps this is why there is sometimes an especially harsh quality about a woman (as opposed to a man) who rejects love. She is more aware of the dangers of giving in to love, of the pain that can and must follow the acceptance of birth.

Bernadette Soubirous had to tell others about the vision that had come to her, the "Lady" who appeared to her in a remote rocky cleft. She longed to keep it to herself, to hug it as her own, but it had to be told; that is the nature of such things. She told it first, as must happen, in order to share, to give it words. Then more telling was demanded of her—and more and more. The happening which had begun as her most intimate bliss now belonged to others as well, to dozens and hundreds and eventually hundreds of thousands, who would misinterpret, misunderstand, twist it, batter it, hate it, or deform it with pious prejudices. She had to accept all that, and not "wash her hands of it." It was still hers, she had to love it and suffer. Otherwise, it could not accomplish its mission. In Bernadette, God was made a person, yet again—a personality to which people could react. The person was the Mother, at a time when the image of the Savior had become dim and distorted by sentimental piety mixed with moral rigorism. The Mother could, at that time, better reflect the glory of the eternal Word for ordinary people. So that was how he was born again—in Bernadette's dutiful, accurate, stubborn and devoted speech. The world met him once more, the Word of Life.

That is the anguish, but the joy is greater. The beloved baby can now be seen, admired, given the tribute he deserves. The mother herself glows with the warmth of the affection given to her baby. She did this! This is her baby! And he needs her, only her. She can *do* things for him—feed, wash, dress, play with him. The child's welfare is her concern and responsibility. The loss of oneness is painful but the ability to form a relationship with another is the result, and it is very precious.

When the Word has been implanted and welcomed, the awareness of a new kind of life to be lived becomes an awareness of a person. It is very hard to describe without distortion, but the experience of motherhood, even the physical possibility of motherhood, helps. For when a person has received God's message, and realized the existence of a new life, after a while it is realized as both inward and outward. There is the sense (hard to realize, it comes with practice) of an abiding core of quietness, an almost painfully, fleetingly glimpsed self, which is yet the same, somehow, as the love, the Word, that has become outward.

The *birth* of this love means being able to recognize it in all kinds of people, as well as in moments of worship. It is visible, touchable; it changes nothing and yet it changes a whole existence, because all the normal things and people, all the usual forms of worship, are now things to which one has given birth in a new kind of life. So the inward, painfully joyful and joyfully painful knowledge is actually one with the loved, served, cherished, newly-born world.

St. Paul (hardly a feminine type) recognized

this womanly aspect of the new life. He said he had given birth to his converts, and when they were troubled and weak in faith he felt as if he had to be in labor all over again, to bring them to birth. It sounds a rather far-fetched metaphor, at first, yet it is true to experience. Every pain and weakness of the child is an inward pain for the mother who has to consent once more to realize that the love she bore is not her own, is not hers to rule, is separate, and yet is still at the heart of her existence, and commands her service and devotion in order to grow as it should.

God in human flesh is Jesus, but is also (since he is the eldest brother) every human person. Each one is brought to birth physically, and must be brought to birth spiritually *by someone* if the humanness is to become itself as the body grows. God in both is at work, in the self that received the Word and gives it birth, in the self which feels the enlivening power of that love, and in his or her turn must recognize God's messenger. It's all very odd, but it isn't just a pious metaphor, it happens, and we can see it happening. It happens with parents and children, but also in marriages where the love of one partner can almost visibly bring a *person* to birth where there seemed only a bundle of reactions and moods. It happens with foster-parents and children and in friendships. It happens often when a young person loves an old, lonely one, or when an old, wise and generous one loves one who is young and rebellious and lonely. It happens when a man or woman discovers that he/she is in love with God, and his/her prayer suddenly achieves what seems to be almost a life of its own, and indeed it is, for it is the life of the Spirit himself, while it is also the person's own life, too. And, in fact, this is what happens in each case, whether particular human relationships are involved or not. In every case, the Spirit of God has taken human form, and comes forth into the world, to work.

IV
Receiving God's Word

When a person discovers God in his/her life, there comes the need to tell someone whom they feel capable of full understanding, as Mary told Elizabeth. She fully intended to tell her and no one else at that time. But, as we saw, the new life grows, and is born, and then it is, in some sense, public. This means that the person who has given it birth can no longer decide whom to tell, or not to tell. People will realize that something new has come into the situation, so unexpected reactions may present themselves.

When Simeon and Anna recognized something special about one particular peasant baby brought to the Temple by his parents, they were showing us something about the way the life of God in man develops. Even if nobody says a thing about it, it is recognizable by those who are sensitive to such things. To most of those who have everyday contact with a person who has received God's Word, nothing important seems to have changed. Perhaps she is observed to spend more time alone, to read "religious" books, take on some special voluntary work. Perhaps she is a little more gentle, more forbearing, more peaceful. Perhaps she even tries to talk about what has happened. Certainly, she's behaving differently, but as far as most people are concerned this is an "extra," she's "turned pious," or "got religion," or she's in a religious phase! Nothing has really changed. But some will be aware of the nature of what has happened, even though she says nothing. Those who are themselves "looking for the consolation of Israel," the coming of God, are quickly aware of the presence of the one they wait for, the Consoler and Savior, carried by some person no one else finds worthy of notice.

It can happen to any of us, one doesn't have to be a saint. The attempt to say "yes" to God, however inadequate and feeble, changes people. God comes into our lives, even if we find this hard to credit. He works there, he becomes, in some degree, available to others who are wanting him. It happens, sometimes, to people who do not believe. They can't name the happening, yet, gropingly, they serve it and live it.

The child is already revealing his proper nature, not by any special missionary impulse on the part of the one who bears the Word of life, but by a wordless communication of power and joy beneath the everyday appearance. The jargon of the youth culture talks of good and bad "vibes," and these "vibrations" of moral and spiritual character are easy to identify but hard to describe. The effect on others of a person who is just normally happy and open is very marked, she can change a roomful of gloom and irritations into a roomful of friendliness and hope. All the more powerful, then, are the "vibrations" of the person who has become aware of the reality at the heart of life and is letting it grow according to its proper nature.

Its nature is to communicate, it cannot be kept private. The message, indeed, is offered by one to another in some such way as the fifteen mysteries symbolize. For some, an apparently chance encounter and recognition, like Simeon's with the child, is part of the message of God for that person. Simeon had lived with God for many years, yet this was a new experience, a new "annunciation," inviting him to receive God's Word into himself, to be born to eternal life. Simeon's earthly life was nearly over, his openness near-total; we can guess that many "invitations" had come to him, and been accepted, and grown to fullness, before this last one. Each one follows the same pattern of growth, because that is its nature, but some are tiny events, some change the course of a whole life, and each is different, none is "routine." Each acceptance makes more likely the coming of further invitations, until the last one, the invitation to die.

In the growth of the Word of God, implanted in a human heart, there is this stage of being available to the sensitive but not obvious to just anyone. It is an experience of great comfort to the people it happens to, it is part of what the idea of "church" implies. Here is a group of people who are, or at any rate might be, "on the same wave-length," even if one has never met them before and has little or no everyday contact. When some Christians long to worship as a "church" of people who know each other and like each other already, they are valuing one kind of good experience, like that of Mary and Elizabeth, whose sharing of joy was made likely and enhanced by their previous knowledge of each other. But there is another kind of experience, just as important in understanding the Spirit's work in mankind, and that is the awed recognition that God has brought together people who have nothing in common except their willingness to do his will.

The Church includes, of course, many people who are Christians because they have been brought up that way, and have stayed with it for one reason or another, but who have not yet reached the point of becoming aware of God's transforming invitation. This is important, for the Church is not just a group of the converted, it is wider than that. But it would be of no use to these others, it could never offer them God's invitation, if it did not include a sizeable number of those who, like Simeon and Anna, are quietly, perseveringly, living in the Spirit, able to be aware of God's comings in others and to identify and praise them.

This recognition by someone else is important. It can be especially important for a woman, at this crucial time in the development of woman's self-consciousness, because many a woman finds it hard to realize just what kind of a person she is, and therefore what kind of thing it is that God is making in her. She is aware of God's life born in her, yet it is still silent, she doesn't yet know how it will grow—how she must help it to grow. There is a danger of stereotypes. The "pious woman" stereotype is waiting to be clamped onto her by many would-be advisers who assume that she will choose the religious life, or some definite outward form of religious activity, prayer-group, etc., as the appropriate way of "training" the God-life she has borne.

At the opposite extreme there is the "liberated" stereotype, the idea that the "new" woman can't possibly do the things women have "normally" done, and should be fired to undertake the cause of women in some sense, to fight injustice and discrimination, help "battered wives," join a women's group, dispensing with the help of males. Again, these may be, and in some cases are, good things to do. The point is that whichever way a woman is pushed, if the pushers are doing it for their own purposes, then they are not trying to help the person to recognize the nature of her own gift. Some people (including some women) want a woman to fit into certain new or old roles because that makes *them* (not the woman) feel safer. Their heavy-handed methods are not likely to help much. But the reverent, humble, matter-of-fact yet intimate recognition of what God is doing in a person really does help.

Simeon's recognition put into words what Mary had obscurely known. He did not tell her what she ought to do, define her role as mother of the Anointed, he simply expressed what he realized was the *nature* of her calling, so that she herself was better able to cope with it. She had to work it out for herself, but he—and Anna—helped her. They neither bullied her nor fawned on her. They didn't interfere yet that moment of recognition was another crucial point in the development of the Word of life that came into the world.

Mary probably never saw either of the two old people again, yet their influence was vital, and the intuition of Christian spirituality, from Luke onward, has sensed that this tiny incident had a symbolic importance almost on a level with the birth itself. That is how much it matters that there should be people of "spiritual discernment" around, to recognize and encourage the new, scarcely articulate growth of the Word.

V
A Spiritual Craving

The movement, the line of growth, continues. It is a beautiful shape. The coming, which develops the need for sharing, in its turn gives confidence to cope with the time of birth (loss and gain at once). Once born, the need to understand inwardly *what* has been born demands deep recognition and understanding. "And Mary kept all these things in her heart," the child kept growing, and there came a time when what was known, in silence and intimately, had to be discovered in a new way, and tested against existing ideas and ways. One has to discover how all this new life fits in with older ways—or doesn't.

The child, coming to the edge of manhood, was feeling the need to know more about himself. The mother, through this, was learning the nature of her own role.

When a person is developing in the Christian life this is an essential stage. We all know some religious people who seem somehow "soft." They are good, kind, genuinely pious yet one feels an indefiniteness that seems to warn, "Don't lean on this person. She may not be strong enough." You wonder how much bone and muscle of spiritual personality there is under the kindness and piety. This is, often enough, due to a sort of spiritual "dietary deficiency." There have been lots of prayer meetings and helpful conversations and hymns and books about prayer or saints new and old, but not much intellectual work. This doesn't mean reading heavy theology, unless one has a taste for it, but it does mean putting her natural intelligence, as well as enthusiasm, to work (hard work) in trying to understand what is going on. What is my calling? How does it mesh with other people's? What kind of thing is this Christian community, Church, or whatever? What is its history, its usefulness? What is it *for*? What am I in it for? In what way is it part of God's plan? How much does my life in this Church depend on what Christians have thought, and done, in past centuries?

People have minds, and if they are to develop spiritually in a full and balanced way they have to use their minds, and give them as much suitable food as they need. Part of this comes by reading, but perhaps even more profound in its effects is talking with others about the big issues—not just religious ones, but political, economic, domestic, psychological ones. The struggle to relate the great things of one's own spiritual growth to all the events and ideas that make up our world is a life-long one. Some need to do more work intellectually than others, and some find it easy and fun (and may over-value it) while for others it is difficult. This may not be because they are un-intellectual types but because they have an uneasy feeling that some of the intellectual ways of solving problems are too glib, too tidy, and miss the greater truth. It is true that the human mind cannot grasp more than the bare skin of truth, never the heart and soul, yet it can help to order, to make experience usable and useful, to prevent feelings taking charge. It can apply general, common moral insights to personal problems, and so clarify them.

The human mind is a beautiful tool. It is limited but it is all we have. To neglect to use it is a kind of spiritual suicide by laziness, and it is one to which women are prone, partly because they have always been told that to cope with spiritual and moral matters intellectually makes them cold and inhuman. It could, of course, but not if mind and heart and spirit work *together.* It is a lot easier to read a religious biography or join in hymn singing than to grapple with harsh moral problems like abortion or pacifism, or try to understand why, and how, and how far, an "institutional" church is necessary. This kind of study and discussion can be worrying and unsatisfying, whereas emotional piety leaves us contented. But then, as Mary found, the calling to bear God into the world involves facing up to the moral and political and religious issues of past and present.

Jesus, the child and Word of God, at the point of accepting manhood, was driven by so intense a need for this intellectual-religious clarification—of what he was, in and of his people, of their calling and his—that he could become oblivious of other needs and loves.

This is the craving of the intellect, but it is a *spiritual* hunger, it is a need for food for the whole person. Until it is to some extent satisfied there can be no proper growth. There is always a need for this mental food, in some degree, but later the appetite changes. Many spiritual people find in later years that they read fewer books, or re-read some, and conversations about religious and other things are surrounded by the feeling that so much *cannot* be said that to have to say anything is almost a burden. But that is because their earlier studies and thinking have become part of themselves. They are not rejected, rather they are absorbed differently. We give extra vitamins to growing children, sometimes, which the full-grown, strong body can get from normal diet without additions.

Many people have abused the intellect by treating it as the only and absolute criterion of human value. It can never be that, but without it we are at the mercy of half-understood moods and prejudices, thrown around by ill-informed enthusiasm, unsteady and impatient and easily discouraged.

The need for mental development in spiritual life was well recognized by St. Benedict and he provided for regular study in his Rule. The great reformer of Carmel, St. Teresa, had no time for feather-headed women. Teresa, the mystic, had a strong sense of the basic importance of intelligence and common sense in Christian life. For, in the end, it isn't just a matter of exercising the mind. If God's Word is forever beyond words, it is still by words that, at first, we communicate with him, share him, understand him and worship him. The way we struggle to express in words, (*together*), what we experience of God's way and life, forms us powerfully as we work at living it. The long labor, through centuries, of expressing what we know is what is called the "tradition" of the Church, and it goes back further still, to the Jewish tradition, which was the "language" of life and worship for all Jews.

The boy Jesus, sitting among other young students of the Torah, heard the great teachers expounding, explaining and debating the Law, the embodiment of an age-old attempt to live according to the will of the Lord for his chosen people. Listening to them must have satisfied a deep longing which the young, fast-growing mind has for "strong" intellectual and spiritual food, something to chew on now that the grown-up world is opening out. He asked them questions, trying to integrate the old wisdom to his own insights and needs, still barely formed. And his mother had to become aware of this new dimension to his life, and accept it, and grow by it herself.

A woman, however "feminine" her nature, has a need to reach out to knowledge, and make it her own. She also has, more easily than a man very often, the sense that this kind of learning must, in a sense, be "taken home" and lived with, before its full meaning can develop. This "living with" what is learned is a great test of its reality. It is very easy to be impressed and enthused by new ideas at first, and few people have the keenness of mind, and wide knowledge, to detect at once a specious, superficial idea, a false though attractive interpretation of life. But if the idea is "taken home" and lived with in among all the good, tested, familiar ones, its value gradually becomes clearer. The "womanly" ability to do this is not, fortunately, confined to women, but men find it harder, partly because our culture is unbalanced and has overemphasized the masculine side of all of us, so intellect and reason are given a final say which they can't cope with. They lead, not to wisdom, but to an insane self-confidence which ignores all evidence that doesn't flatter its own achievements.

It was right that the boy Jesus, the Word growing and craving new food, should reach out beyond the confines of home, should seek and find contact with mature, informed minds, and grow and stretch in the thrill of debate and argument, exulting in this wonderful world of a whole people's wisdom. It was right, also, that the child should return to his home and his mother, and live with the new learning, in the familiar ways and places, and compare one with the other, and let each change the other in his mind and in his mother's mind.

There is no going back. The early time of spiritual awakening is beautiful and profoundly moving, it has little need to question or intellectualize. But the day has to come when it needs more, and if this is denied it ceases to grow, it becomes unbalanced and uneasy and self-indulgently emotional or just fades away. But the new challenge is not a loss of innocence, it is a necessary development, and the deep, real innocence—the "single eye"—judges the new experience, sifts and sorts it, and draws to itself, as St. Paul says, "what is holy, and just, and good."

VI
The Final Stage of Growth

The five joyful mysteries show us the coming of God's Word into the world through the response of one woman, first of all. They show the stages of growth, and they are stages in all spiritual growth. They happen to every human being who receives God's message with a sincere heart, as they happened to Mary, in the beginning. The stages may overlap, and take different forms, but they are all part of the process by which God forms himself in humankind, in the historical coming of Jesus, and in the many comings which that made possible.

These five happenings are intimate, individual, they are identifiable psychological stages in a person who welcomes the message. The five mysteries that follow, the ones we call sorrowful, are not like this. They are not successive happenings in the sense that they have to happen in that order and that way, as they happened to Jesus. Rather, they show us from different aspects the meaning of the death of Jesus, and through him the meaning of death for everyone and for the whole people, a meaning changed beyond all expectation by that one particular death.

Death is a necessity, if God's work is to reach its perfection. The New Testament repeats this over and over again, in metaphor, in direct statement, and supremely in the accounts of the passion of Jesus. The life that has grown from the moment of acceptance, that has given itself in service and love, has to die before it can be completed. And this can happen over and over again, for the "dying" of the old self is not complete in one single oblation in normal human lives. The liberated new self is real, but there are still areas of the self not yet transformed, not yet dead—and risen. And of course it all comes to completion with physical death, yet that death is prepared—even, in a sense, undergone—in the earlier stages of earthly living. In the five mysteries of the passion of Jesus we recognize the way it has to be, in all human beings, yet the rosary is especially our Lady's prayer, and this allows us to look for the special teaching which lies in these "mysteries" for women, but also for the wisdom of the feminine side of all human beings.

The agony of Jesus before his passion is perhaps the moment of deepest humiliation, for it is the moment of fear, the moment when the realization of suffering has found no hope, no strength, to make it supportable. It is the moment—a long, timeless moment—of disintegration, because the usual supports suddenly are not there. There is no way out, no one to turn to, the interior resources which have helped in the past are now useless. Jesus, lying on his face in the grass, is an image of this position of total helplessness. Our hindsight tells us that strength will come, courage will come, but the whole horror of this moment is that at the time there is no assurance of this, only emptiness and a horror of uncontrollable fear. It isn't so much fear of some particular, foreseen pain, as a kind of clinging, blinding garment, close bandages that make the least movement of heart and mind impossible. There is nothing but fear.

The old song says that "men must work and women must weep," and it is indeed the feminine side of a person that has to cope with the kind of suffering that has no option of activity to relieve the pain. Such danger and pain, mental or physical, are imposed by forces the person cannot control and cannot fight. There is no way to shorten or relieve it, but only to pass through it all, somehow or other. This is the pain of motherhood—not so much the physical pain of childbirth, which is mainly an unnecessary pain imposed by the artificial attitudes and phobias of over-civilized living, but the pain of a love which can only avoid hurt by destroying the bond, the love itself. Some women do. They cannot face the agony of their children's failures, sins and sorrows, so they thrust the erring child out of their hearts, erect a wall of bitterness to keep out the suffering. It is the emotional equivalent to the way in which a desperate woman may abandon her illegitimate baby, or even kill it. The agony of responsibility for the child's future is too great, so the child is rejected. The older parent, too, who rejects the child because of his or her behavior is, in a sense, killing the "child within." But the woman who refuses to kill the child within must suffer the consequences, and that means she must suffer all that goes wrong with her child's life, and generally there is not much she can do about what goes wrong *except* suffer.

In a wider sense, the womanly side of human nature suffers in this way all kinds of human pain and sin. In the villages of storm-beaten coasts, when a wreck was sighted it was the men who went out, at great peril, to try to rescue the survivors. The women stayed at home, ready with blankets and food and bandages, but with no absorbing activity to fill their minds and deaden their feelings while they waited, holding in their hearts the danger of their husbands and sons and the fear and pain of the shipwrecked. "Men must work and women must weep," and this kind of weeping is not weakness, but can be redemptive; it is the profound acceptance, without bitterness or rebellion, which can transform the world's agony into the world's salvation. It involves a kind of deep courage which doesn't feel like courage, but consists simply in a refusal to reject, to surrender to panic, to take refuge from pain in empty activity.

Out of this deep and agonizing acceptance comes the possibility of action which is also redemptive, and indeed the two can happen together in time as when a mother nurses a sick child. It is a demanding and skilled and exhausting task which is not an escape but a companion to the agony of passive acceptance of the fact that there is no control over life and death, that the best one can do may not be enough. But the agony of Jesus symbolizes the helplessness, the acceptance of the intolerable, the pain of doing nothing.

There is a certain time in a woman's life when this kind of "weak" courage is especially needed. It is not a time of crisis, it may not be marked by any special sorrows or trials. It is a time when all that has been achieved through years of child-bearing and rearing, or through the building up of a career, or the creation of a power of service to others, begins to seem questionable. For years the work itself gives meaning and purpose to life, but after a long time little doubts enter. I have achieved, I have done my best for these children, I have succeeded in my career, I have given help and devotion and it has been visibly worthwhile. I have reached a kind of plateau after long struggle. Where do I go now? What does it all mean?

Jesus worked and preached and prayed, proclaiming the good news, calling men and women to conversion and new life, and they flocked to him and loved him. Yet one day the whole achievement was useless, he was alone, and nothing he had done, nobody he had loved and served, was of any use or support to him. It was, literally, undone. That realization of the final uselessness of all that we can do—of the very best that we can do—in the face of the power of evil, is the essence of this initial agony of the passion.

It is one that comes to most women, though to some later than others, for a very useful and satisfying life can postpone the realization until old age reduces the physical ability to be of use in the accustomed way. Sometimes, indeed, it is the approach of death itself which pulls away the structure of achievement. The need to come to terms with the loss of all that made the person seem real and meaningful is one of the most painful parts of the necessary preparation for death. Doctors and others who have nursed the terminally sick, and helped them prepare for death, have emphasized the crucial nature of this moment of truth, when the clothing of achievement is pulled off, and the person must deal with his or her own naked self, facing the greatest transition of all.

But even if this moment comes at a much earlier stage of life it is still part of the approach to death. It is the time when the person must, as it were, face round toward the end and begin to realize the rest of life in relation to death, and not in relation to external achievement. To women with children this moment often comes naturally when they grow up, and one kind of usefulness is coming to an end. There may be years of even greater usefulness ahead, but it will only be *real* usefulness if it is made facing death. If it is simply an attempt to fill the void, to escape the confrontation with the "useless" self (the one which must encounter the transition of death) then there is great danger of becoming possessive, domineering, an interfering busybody. A woman like this is the kind of person relations dread to invite, because she is silently or openly critical of how others do things, always wants to do it herself, or else continually explains how busy and expert she once was.

It is hard to abandon one kind of usefulness, to accept "the lower place" at the table of human achievement, to let others take over cherished roles, to watch them making mistakes, and not interfere. It is a kind of death, and it is essential. It is only by fully accepting the pain of this—often prolonged—purgation that a woman can enter the latter part of her life creatively, in a state of spiritual integrity and peace.

At the end of his agony, "angels ministered" to Jesus, bringing him peace and courage to face what lay ahead. This came *after* the agony, which had to be endured uncomforted and alone. It is always so. This is a lonely struggle and part of its nature is due to the realization of aloneness. No matter how many loving people are around, wanting to help, they can do nothing. This must be done alone.

It can be done. It is done year after year by millions of ordinary women who learn—without ever putting it into words—to say "not as I will but as Thou wilt," to accept the loss of what has made life meaningful, and to face around and go forward peacefully to whatever is demanded of them.

What lies ahead may be years of happy fulfillment, before death comes close in physical reality, and the rest of the process of dying has to be coped with. The passion of Jesus shows us the act of dying telescoped into a short space of time, but however the stages are spaced out, they have to be undergone—or else rejected.

The willingness to accept fully the earlier "preparation" for death makes the end of life fuller, more whole—and more useful. The peace that follows the agony envelops not only the sufferer but all her little world. It is part of the world's redemption.

VII
A Means Toward Freedom

On the whole, women are better at bearing pain than men. They make less fuss when they are ill, and don't regard their ailments as an outrageous insult from a malignant Fate. Of course this is not a general rule; there are plenty of quietly courageous men and plenty of spoiled, self-pitying women, and one kind of masculine-dominated culture has almost required women to be weak and querulous, so that men can feel superior to them. But, overall, it is true that the ability to bear pain, and go on bearing it, with an almost stolid endurance, is more often a feminine characteristic. The masculine ideal of courage is, rather, an active one, symbolized by the warrior, fearless in battle and indifferent to danger and wounds.

This is why the suffering of the passion of Jesus has a special significance for the proper development of the feminine side of every human psyche. Psyche, the Soul, is indeed a feminine concept, and her suffering in the myth of Psyche is the long, painful, lonely journey in search of her lost beloved. This kind of suffering is endured for the sake of the beloved, and nothing else matters. There is nothing, here, of the stoic pride of the one who will not give in because that would be an admission of personal weakness. Personal weakness, in fact, is the essence of Psyche's pain as she struggles on to accomplish a quest which seems far beyond her strength, but which *must* be accomplished, for the sake of the one who is loved.

The Beloved of Christ, the Bride of scriptural symbolism, is every redeemed soul. In an odd way, the symbolism is reversed, in the passion of Jesus, for it is Psyche, the feminine Soul, who endures in order to save. In the Old Testament, the Wisdom of God is the divine influence at work in the world, and Wisdom is feminine. We see here how the man Jesus, the whole, perfect human being, shows the fullness of development of both the masculine and feminine sides of human nature. He is "the Word and Wisdom" of God, the feminine Psyche who suffers and saves.

On the feasts of our Lady, lessons taken from passages about the divine Wisdom are often used, and applied to her. We understand this better when we consider the mysteries of her assumption and coronation, but already we can see a little why she has always been so important in Catholic spirituality. At times when the idea of God was an overwhelmingly masculine one, her presence at the heart of the mystery of the incarnation kept alive the sense of the "feminine" aspect of God's work of salvation. The Word and Wisdom of God are incarnate in Jesus, but take flesh through Mary, the two intimately linked in physical relationship but also symbolically. In pictures of the crucifixion, the figure of Mary is used to reflect and intensify the sense of the suffering of Jesus. Although she is not physically present at some scenes of the passion, she is emotionally and symbolically present, in a very important way, at every stage. The rosary is her prayer, and the repeated "Hail, Mary" keeps this awareness just beneath but close to our conscious minds as we consider the mysteries. In this second scene, a scene of sheer brutality, unchecked by compassion or even by the limits of harsh justice, we can be aware of the outrage more deeply through the feminine type of consciousness; in Mary the woman, and in Jesus himself, Psyche is on her painful pilgrimage for love's sake.

We are considering one of the most basic and crude kinds of human evil, the deliberate infliction of damage to the body of a human being, not in self-defense or in war, not in the heat of anger, but as a punishment inflicted by the powerful on the powerless, mainly as a demonstration of that power. "I am the master. You have dared to do something that throws doubt on my mastery. I will demonstrate that mastery by what I can do to your body, and you cannot prevent it." That is the message conveyed by this kind of judicial brutality, a punishment whose purpose is much more to demonstrate total power than to redress the balance upset by crime. The power of Rome had to be absolute; any hint of refusal to submit had to be crushed totally. The same principle has underlain the "justice" of many powerful states, and still inspires the penal practices of our own time.

To give just one example—during the last war, four men of the Hutterite sect, who are pacifists by religious conviction, refused to obey the draft. They were imprisoned, beaten, left naked in subzero temperatures, hung up by their arms, deprived of food, and constantly mocked and abused. All four eventually died of this treatment, and as a final insult were buried in the uniforms they had refused to wear living. The abuse of judicial power is not ancient history.

To the extent to which we accept such a system, and assent to the deliberate physical degradation and torture of men and women who break the codes of our society, we are represented by the soldiers who carried out, and watched, the scourging of Jesus. They were "only obeying orders," they would have said. They were behaving and reacting as their society expected them to behave and react. There is a side to all of us that all too easily finds a "legal" excuse for indulging hatred and the desire to destroy anyone whose ideas (or even existence) challenges our settled prejudices.

We do this because we are afraid. We cannot bear the pain of discovering that some of our favorite prejudices are unsound. Pilate could not face the notion that there might be another dimension to life, beyond the power-play of Rome and her subjects. It was easier to pretend not to see the challenge, and to fit the case into the category of "rebellion." We all do it sometimes. Mothers do it when their children ask questions that are too searching, or, by their actions, pose even deeper moral questions. Instead of trying to make an honest answer, we crush the questioner by sheer adult authority.

We need to change sides, to shift from the position of power to the position of weakness and humiliation. That is what the passion of Jesus challenges us to do. It is perhaps easier for a woman to grasp imaginatively what the scourging means, because the care of human bodies is most often the woman's work, and the wounding of the body is an attack on her vocation of nurture and healing. It is hard to accept; the natural reaction is a huge anger, a desire to fight back. Sometimes that is the right way, the necessary thing. But there is this to consider: traditional Christian spirituality has concentrated on the passion and death of Jesus as the moment of redemption, because the insight that death is not only the condition of, but in a sense "contains," resurrection is uniquely and supremely the Christian truth. But it is easy to overlook something essential to this, which is that the person who died had first to live. What was un-made, in order to be transformed, had first to be made—in the womb, in the home, growing up to manhood, physically and intellectually and spiritually. Mary was in great degree responsible for that making—therefore the un-making, when it came, was an attack on the whole meaning and purpose of her life. She had to feel that in the depth of herself, and accept the un-making of the mother and healer in her, so that these might be transformed into something more perfect, not obliterating them but transforming them.

Nevertheless it was, it is, a horror and an outrage. We are right to be horrified and outraged at what human beings do to the bodies of other human beings. We have to live that horror, and live through it. It is going on all over the world in prisons and military detention centers, in homes where children are abused, in "nursing homes" for the old where the residents are too weak and afraid to protest their treatment. For all these bodies, there has to be a "motherhood" that is aware of outrage. Thus it can—mysteriously, uncomforted—

work the transformation, which can happen because there is oneness. There is one body, which is Christ's, one motherhood, which is Mary's, yet it is also his, and his body is hers, and ours.

VIII
The Crown of Victory

In the Gospel accounts of the events of Jesus' life, the evangelists often record that people do or say things whose meaning is not apparent at the time, or to themselves. When the evangelists record that the possessed hailed Jesus as "Son of God" they did not mean to suggest that these afflicted people grasped the full sense of the title, but that their use of it symbolized the way the powers of evil recognized the true nature of their enemy. When Caiaphas said that it was right that "one man should die that the whole people perish not," he presumably meant that it was better to execute one man than risk a rebellion, and the retribution of Rome, but "being High Priest for that year" his words had in the record of the evangelist a cosmic significance he could never have intended.

In the same way, the crowning of Jesus with thorns by the Roman guard was a bit of barrack-room humor of an extremely "sick" variety, at the expense of a man from a conquered people, a legitimate butt for brutality. But that sadistic joke has become a treasured symbol of the victory of the Christ, who overcame pain and death by undergoing them and rules by that sign—the sign of the kingship of love "even unto death." This symbol has become so closely linked in our minds with the suffering and victorious Christ that almost all pictures of the crucifixion, from at least the fourteenth century onward, show Jesus on the cross wearing the crown of thorns, although there is no indication of this in the Gospel accounts. It seems unlikely, on the face of it, that the crown of thorns would have been replaced after Jesus' "own garments" were given back to him; the private soldiers' barrack-room jest might not have been approved by the officers in charge. But whatever the historical fact, the symbolic power of that horrible crown is great, and its constant use in art shows how much it means to Christians.

From the point of view of the inward transformation of the person symbolized by these mysteries, the crowning of Jesus indicates the reason for the sense of awe and reverence that many people feel in the presence of suffering bravely borne. When Ann Frank, after the years of hiding with her family from the Nazis, was finally captured and taken to a concentration camp, someone who saw her there survived to record the impression she made on her fellow prisoners. Emaciated, ill, shaven, and half naked, the Jewish teenager had about her a "radiance," said the observer. Her courage did not falter, and her compassion and care for others was constant—a much more unusual thing. The ending of this brief life, a pathetic failure of early promise from the worldly point of view, was in fact an heroic achievement. The "radiance" of her face, which seems to have been actually visible, was the sign of her conquest; she was truly "crowned," and the reverence which others felt was the kind of reverence felt for awesome power. We can realize the sense of the phrase "the martyr's crown." It isn't just a conventional sign; it corresponds to the feeling people have about heroic suffering.

I once knew a woman—she was about fifty at the time—who had been in bed since her girlhood with a painful and progressive illness. Part of her ailment involved having a drain permanently in her side, so she could not move much even in bed, and was in more or less constant pain, sometimes less and sometimes more. I knew this from those who nursed her, and also that she seldom had a restful night. From her own words and behavior one would never have guessed anything of the kind, for she talked about what concerned her visitors, about the birds that fed from the bird-table by her window, or the changing trees outside, or books she had read. She was always cheerful and often funny and interesting, for she read widely. She didn't talk about her spiritual life either, except to express gratitude for the kindness of the priest who brought her Holy Communion twice a week, and sometimes celebrated Mass in her room—a rare treat for her. Glimpses of it appeared, however, in her conversation, for her sense of joy and gratitude for life and its gifts was constant. Once, she admitted that at one time she had fought furiously against her fate, had felt bitter and rebellious. That time was past and those who visited her—there were many—came away with a memory of good conversation and fun, and a feeling of peace and joy, but also with a little of that reverence which is symbolized by the crown of thorns, the royalty of suffering fully accepted and thus transformed.

We easily think of religiously accepted suffering as rather self-conscious and uncomfortable to live with. When we talk of a "martyred" attitude we mean someone who uses her suffering (real or imaginary) to dominate and impress others. And there is also the fact that in the early stages a person who is trying hard to come to terms with suffering, recognizing it as God's way of salvation, often *is* rather self-conscious about it. There is a conscious effort, not always successful, and it shows, and it makes others feel uncomfortable. But if the struggle is maintained, in the end the self-consciousness fades. The accepted suffering becomes part of the whole personality, a means toward spiritual freedom and peace, even joy. It is not at all "martyrish" in the unpleasant sense, but creates that feeling of power, a kind of royalty of the spirit, in which others feel safe, cherished and supported.

This isn't an uncommon experience. There are a good many women who never think of themselves as anything special at all, but who have coped with unhappy marriages, or bad health, or bereavement, or poverty, or several of these, and have not become embittered but have transformed the pain into that royalty which helps to establish the kingdom of heaven on a little bit of earth. They have a kind of dignity of soul which can go quite well with ungainliness of body or even of mind. In relation to them, the phrase "noblesse oblige" loses its atmosphere of condescending grandeur, and means that the kind of nobility which comes from fully lived suffering releases in the person a power to love and to serve which can be tapped in no other way.

A crown is visible to others, not to the one

who wears it, once it is in place. It is a glory that others recognize and reverence; the bearer of the crown never sees it. To her it is only thorns, a pain which, she feels, she bears very badly. The wearer can, of course, see a crown reflected in a mirror, but there is only one kind of mirror that reflects this crown, and that is the face of another person also crowned. The saints saw it first and most clearly on the head of Christ, and also on the head of his mother. Seeing it, they do not know that they are seeing themselves. They only worship that which they feel helpless to emulate—you *have* to feel helpless to wear this crown. (Jesus was.) Sometimes wearers of this crown see it on the head of a friend, and recognize its meaning with awe and joy, being especially sensitive to such things. It is one of the most touching and even funny experiences to hear one such everyday saint, visibly wearing the crown of thorns, expressing her own reverence for the crown worn by another. If anyone tries to tell her about her own she becomes impatient, embarrassed, even rather angry at such a suggestion.

Bernadette of Lourdes had a life so full of many kinds of mental and physical pain that it hurts to read about it. The one thing that made her really angry was praise. Her whole life was a reflection of the glory she had seen, and she knew it was a glory gained through suffering. Her own suffering seemed to her a trivial everyday task which she had to work at, since God had nothing better for her to do. Others saw her crown; she never did. She is probably one of the greatest of saints, but we tend to take her at her own valuation, as merely an instrument, used and then put away. But her "uselessness" made a mirror to reflect the power of the victory of Christ's passion. In the end she was nothing but a mirror, a perfect image of the crowned Christ. She never knew it; none of them ever does. That is the nature of such a crown.

IX

The Path to Calvary

One kind of pain that has come to mothers of young adults in recent years has been the pain of seeing them embrace ideals which appear to challenge the inherited values which their parents cherish. Boys and girls "drop out" and reject their parents' way of life, and often their religion. Often their motives are mixed, there is much ignorance, much lack of judgment, much misplaced enthusiasm, and a good deal of laziness and fear. But there is also idealism, and hope, and the parents of such young people have to learn to distinguish, to cherish the genuine courage and idealism, and help the rest to fall away in time. But if such parents do try to support their children in their ventures, and help them to sort out the real from the phony, the good from the shoddy, they will share in society's condemnation of the children's behavior. They may be ostracized, even legally penalized. They will lose friends, and suffer from malignant gossip and petty persecution. It is all part of the passion, the dying. It is their own dying, and by it they also help their children to discover the genuine ideals, and set aside what is self-indulgent, or merely angry, or lazily optimistic.

Public blame is easiest to bear if one can manage to despise the persecutors, and there are usually plenty of excuses for despising the narrow-minded, fear-ridden, hate-filled people who condemn any new and challenging idea and will go to violent lengths to crush the unfamiliar. The angry, brutalized crowds who mocked Christ staggering under the weight of the cross are very familiar to anyone who has tried to live by the ideals their contemporaries do not share, or who has even dared to express sympathy with those who are trying different ways.

Yet to return hate for hate, to despise the despisers, is to distort the effort to find a better way. It is easy to reject what is false out of pride, and even to suffer for it. It is hard to keep to what one sees as the right way, without compromise, but without hate. In recent years, many Catholics have become embittered because they seemed to get little sympathy or support when they tried, as it seemed to them, to find better ways to bring the Gospel message to their contemporaries. They were sometimes condemned by their pastors and accused of all kinds of things. Some left the Church in anger and frustration, and even "lost their faith." From the other point of view, more traditional Catholics felt themselves despised and isolated by the intolerance and sweeping condemnations of "new style" Catholics. Each side saw the other as the enemy, to be defeated or, at best, ignored. So neither learned anything from the other. Neither looked at the face of prejudice and intolerance and saw behind it a fear of losing what was valuable, or a longing for something real yet out of reach. Neither looked beyond the persecution and loved the persecutor. Both, too often, carried their crosses with arrogance, and so made them weapons of war, not instruments of atonement.

To keep one's integrity, to go on searching for what is true and right in spite of the pressure of public opinion, is something Christians have to do, but they have to do it with love. Nowadays, some Christians are looking for new ways of "giving flesh" to the Gospel message, though indeed they turn out to be very traditional ways. Community life, hospitality, simplicity of life-style, a rejection of the profit motive—these ideals are as old as the Church, and they are being expressed in new ways now. Thomas Merton, before he died, hoped that a newer kind of religious community might grow up, which had at its heart a celibate group of people permanently dedicated to a life of prayer, but which could include in its life married people, and families, and others who belonged to it for long or short periods, sharing its life and ideals in varying ways and degrees. There are, by now, a number of such communities and there are other groups, trying in different ways to find a way of life that is properly human, in a society that has lost its way spiritually. This kind of venture is hard in itself, hard physically and psychologically and spiritually, but it is a cross taken up willingly and carried as a way of salvation. It is made harder by the misunderstanding and persecution that often attend it. The most frequent accusation is that such people "don't work," or are sexually immoral, or unpatriotic. Those who hold such opinions cling to them in the face of all evidence, and some communities have actually been driven out by this kind of persecution, their homes burned and their persons assaulted. It is hard not to defend oneself against such hatred by despizing the attackers, by rejection, by isolating oneself from the world which refuses the message. But the carrying of the cross is *essentially* painful, it is public, it is surrounded by abuse and scorn, and yet it must never be carried as a sign of rejection. It must, on the contrary, be a symbol of reconciliation, and must show willingness to receive help, however small, even help without real understanding, even rather patronizing help. The motives for helping are not our affair, we accept thankfully the offer of any Cyrenian who comes along.

To be oneself the Cyrenian, the helper of the cross-bearer, is one way of sharing in the passion, as I suggested earlier. The one who helps receives the same treatment as the one who needs help. The figure of Simon from Cyrene, an unknown foreign visitor who just happened to be around, is of great importance, for it shows how *casual* God's way of working can appear. I can get involved in the needs of others without ever really intending to, just by yielding to a momentary sympathy. Before I know where I am, I am part of the procession to Calvary. This tells us something about the way we become committed to relationships. Young people often marry in great ignorance of each other, and after a while realize what they have taken on. At *that* moment comes the real choice—to accept the burden and bear it, and perhaps discover the glory ahead, or to reject it, saying "But I didn't understand, I was too young." We are always "too young," we never fully understand what we undertake. We will have to make the choice of carrying deliberately what we picked up without much thought.

It's the same, often, with a baby. "Unplanned" babies are, to some people, necessarily also unwanted. They shouldn't be born because they were not deliberately chosen. Life isn't like that. A pregnancy may begin without intention, "accidentally," but already a relationship exists; so then the mother has a choice—to take up the burden willingly, however much she may be afraid and doubtful of her courage and competence, or to reject the demand, saying "away with him"—that is, for me he doesn't exist, let him die, "crucify him."

The final temptation of a person who has willingly taken up a heavy load and is doing her best to carry it, is self-pity, and there are always people around, like the "women of Jerusalem" to offer the kind of sympathy that feeds self-pity. The forms of it are familiar, "Fancy being tied to a man like that," or "After all you've done, to see them behave so ungratefully," and even "It doesn't seem right, a good woman like you, to have so little reward." It is tempting to agree, to feel a glow of self-pity, a little resentment at having to bear so unfair a share of the world's evil. It is easy to forget that the carrying of evil, willingly, is the only way to turn it inside out and make it the stuff of resurrection. It is not the cross-bearer who is to be pitied, deliberately taking on a share of the work of salvation, in a matter-of-fact, day-to-day manner. The ones who are to be pitied are the ones who can't realize the meaning and purpose of such a burden, who spend their lives trying to avoid trouble and end up miserable and afraid. They must indeed weep for themselves and their children.

X

The Mystery of Death

However you look at it, whatever way you interpret it, the end of human life is death. There are a few people who are so wholly prepared for death, so stripped of attachment to inessentials, so unconcerned about themselves, that the transition seems scarcely more than a confirmation of something already known. Some people go gently and eagerly into eternity as if going home after a troublesome journey. But most of us aren't like that. We put off thinking about death as long as we possibly can. We are afraid even to mourn too much the deaths of other people, in case we give death a foothold in our own lives. We don't let children attend funerals, and we lie to them about the fate of relatives who are suddenly no longer there. As a society we are afraid of death; it is the forbidden subject. That is because we belong to an age that has nearly persuaded itself that it can cure *all* evils, given the chance and money for research. Miracle cures, miracle seeds, space exploration, heart transplants. If we can't cure it this year, then next. Except death. Death is our point of failure, and because we can't prevent death we are made aware of all the other things we can't prevent either—hatred, senility, idiocy, for instance. Ironically, our suggested cure for these is death: death for the criminal, death for the incurable (call it "euthanasia") and death for cases of "severe retardation"—before birth if possible. It seems strange that we should want to use death as a weapon against our own death, but so it is. By eliminating the human reminders of mortality we can put off thinking about death—for good, with any luck. The usual idea of the best way to die is "to go to sleep and not wake up"—that is, you don't know anything about it. We try to avoid letting sick people know when death is near—"to spare them," we say, but really because to talk about it to them would force us to think about it ourselves, and their possible fear and loneliness would rouse the ghosts of the same fear and loneliness in ourselves.

In complete opposition to this, Catholics put up crucifixes in their churches and homes, stating symbolically but quite clearly that death, this particular and revolting death, was and is an event of supreme importance, and—finally—one of joy. There it is, up on the wall, and even if it seems to be mainly a place to stick a rather dusty piece of palm, the fact that it is there at all is a witness against us, if we slip into the pervasive habit of mind that refuses to deal with the reality and significance of death. I read recently an article about how Christian white people once treated their black slaves. It's an old and disgraceful story. This particular article was written by a black person, who pointed out that even though these Christians failed so terribly to apply their religious conviction to their treatment of black people, *they had to try hard not to apply it.* They had to find all kinds of excuses—black people weren't "able to manage their own lives," or weren't fully human, etc. This is important, for, after all, the history of slavery shows that most cultures had no bad conscience at all about owning and exploiting slaves. The Greeks and Romans based their whole culture on slave owning, and felt no humanitarian qualms, because there was nothing in their religion to give them any. Christians, however inadequate, had a command of brotherhood, compassion and service laid on them. In the end they ran out of excuses and expedients; their hypocrisy was exposed. In the same way, the crucifix on our walls, the doctrine of atonement in our faith, the theme of the cross in spiritual writings and in the liturgy, are always undermining our attempts to avoid the Christian meaning of death. If we are lucky, our evasions will fail, and we shall have to face facts before death itself faces us in physical reality.

Perhaps it is easier, in some ways, for women to face death, because there are so many times in the lives of ordinary women when they have to face loss—loss of independence when children come, loss of the children, loss of beauty (which our society has made into a major disaster akin to death), loss of the capacity for child-bearing (in itself an important kind of "dying," even for a woman who has had no children, or is dedicated to a celibate life).

The "little deaths" can be evaded; we can pretend there is no real demand on us. We can cling to the freedom of girlhood, refusing the surrender to the needs of the children. We can cling to the children, refusing to allow them to grow up. We can cling to beauty with hair tints and treatments and the wearing of youthful clothes. We can pretend that the menopause is "really" only the end of the nuisance of monthly periods. None of it will make us happy. There are few more pathetic sights than an elderly woman, highly made up, in a dress that exposes her fat knees, bulgy arms and wrinkled elbows, drinking and dancing and "having a good time." Whom does she think she's kidding? The "good time" is a way of so filling up the days that there is no time to realize failure—the basic failure to *live* the successive "dyings" and so change them into life "more abundantly." One woman who suffered in a Russian prison recorded that she came through this experience of torture and near despair, with her faith and love unbroken, because she learned to *let herself experience* the pain. She did not fight it as an enemy, trying to keep it "outside" herself. She let it in; she let the pain be *herself*. It was still pain—worse pain, perhaps, unrelieved by the compensation of hatred and anger. But it was a redemptive pain. She became aware, gradually, that by refusing to hate the men who tortured her she was actually creating a relationship with them—a redemptive relationship. That is the whole mystery; that is what the cross is about.

We have to let death in, let it be ourselves, not hate it. It is still frightening, as the unknown and painful always is, but it is a fear we can cope with. Some of the old prayer books used to tell the good Christian to "compose oneself as for death" on retiring. This isn't as morbid as it sounds. It could be a bit of gruesome fantasy, giving oneself pious shivers, but taken the right way it is simply a daily reminder that death is part of living. The cells of my body die in their millions every day, and the replacement rate decreases. From the moment I reach physical maturity, I begin the long physical descent, the slow disintegration of physical powers. This is simply a fact, and I might as well get used to it. For a Christian, it is a fact of supreme importance, because the crucifixion of Jesus is the event, and the sign, that overcomes death. The final unmaking is the necessary condition of a re-making, a transformation which is beyond imagining, yet does not break the truth of the essential eternal Self. That Self, like the seed in the ground, dies only to spring to new and perfect life.

But the dying is real. The pain and the loss and the grief are real. The destruction is not a mere shedding of an outworn layer; it is the un-making of the person, the whole person, so that the Self may be born. That is the whole mystery. It is a matter of everyday experience; death presents itself to us in little and big ways every day of our lives. If we refuse it and evade it, we shall die just the same, but it will be a barren, hateful death. If we let it in, it will hurt, but we shall live, and others will live by us.

XI
A Healed and Healing Heart

The strange pattern of salvation traces itself in everyday human events, and we have seen some of it. We have seen, especially, the line of the Spirit's path as it is traced in the feminine aspect of human life. Because women have been abused, and their special spiritual capacities used as means to suppress them, it is tempting for women to refuse to allow the significance of the specially feminine role in salvation. Because women have a particular "instinctive" capacity for quietly bearing grief and pain and letting it work in them, they have been labeled "passive" and therefore inferior to the active, masculine element. But because a gift is abused, that does not devalue it. The feminine capacity for assenting to and bringing forth the Word, and then for letting go the thing nurtured and loved, seeing it undone—all this belongs to the essence of the *human* spiritual growth. It must happen in men as well, though it is symbolically a woman's role. Mary is the mother, and she is the symbol of the woman, the bride, the feminine principle for all. So if women fail to accept the feminine role, symbolically and really, there is no symbol to give life to the feminine in men.

It works the other way, of course. Women need to recognize in the "masculine" spirituality the challenge to their own masculine side, which must balance and perfect the feminine side.

Women must strive for that clarity of judgment, that willingness to oppose evil whatever the cost, that undaunted and joyous courage, that willingness to lead and even push others in the right way when necessary, which belong symbolically to the masculine in human nature, and which one can also see in practice in the life of Jesus.

We have seen, in considering the joyful and sorrowful mysteries, that they symbolize and illuminate stages and aspects of spiritual growth in men and women. The sorrowful mysteries, as we saw, are not so much a sequence of stages of growth as symbols of different aspects of one event, the death of the Christ, the death of the human person, and its meanings. With the glorious mysteries there is a difference, again. The first three can be seen as a kind of sequence, in the sense that there is a chain of cause and effect, yet (as theologians tell us) they are essentially *one* event. And in a sense the last two are part of the same event, but they have to be considered separately in order to make clear some things that have historically been neglected in understanding the scheme of salvation.

If one wishes to grasp in a very precise way the significance of the resurrection, there is a kind of experiment one can do. It needs a little solitude, a little uninterrupted period of time, because it demands freedom of mind and heart from other preoccupations. It also needs a little bit of garden, or park, or countryside, or a baby in a crib, or anything else that is growing and alive, even a geranium in a pot. In that quiet and solitude, faced with a thing that is live and growing, think for a while that all this is futile. The leaves will grow and then die; so will the baby. There will be others, all living a little while and then dying. Life on earth is a meaningless, futile, closed cycle of birth and growth and death, in which people invent meanings in order to comfort their hopeless days. Think this, imagine it as fully and really as possible, be convinced of it in imagination, just as if you were a novelist getting "into the skin" of a totally cynical, hopeless person. See how this affects the way you *look* at the growing thing, and how *it* looks to you. It can seem almost hateful, in its silly optimistic growing. "Doom" is written on every leaf and petal, on the baby's cheek.

Then, withdraw your mind from that cycle of despair, let it "rest" a moment, as far as possible. Now look again, and say to yourself, "Christ is risen." The plants and the baby will die, but death is not the meaning of them. Their promise is a real promise, what they symbolize is true. Spring, birth, are not sick jokes but truthful statements of an eternal hope. Autumn and winter are gentle nurses, keeping the spring safe until there is no more need for them. Death, "the last enemy," will die also, and is no longer cruel, but only sad and fleeting. The final reality is not death but life. Look at the delicate outlines of leaf-veins, the curve of grass, the texture of the child's skin, the spring of the lashes. They have a new meaning now, and their meaning makes them *look* different. They are not a cheat, they are true, and painfully beautiful—painful, because there is still death, but beautiful with a promise that death cannot cancel.

Perhaps this sounds fanciful, a kind of forcing

of the imagination. If you try it, you will find that it seems a very "natural" thing to do, for indeed we constantly experience how our state of mind changes the "look" of things around us. But the assertion of resurrection is the assertion that the "bad" moods are liars, and we can and should fight them. We are not simply avoiding the unpleasant when we assert life as the final statement. We are saying what is true, accepting the evidence around us as reliable. Then we realize that the hopeful and positive state of mind is what it seems at the time—the proper and truthful one.

The Gospel accounts of the risen life of Jesus, and Christian thought about it, have "felt" the resurrection—ascension as one "movement" of transformation. They belong together, they are "the return to the Father," but we can realize two parts, not just in the accounts of the evangelists but in our own experience of learning that life is the meaning of life. The first is indicated by my little experiment. The risen Christ is, as St. Paul says "the first born among many brethren," and also the whole process of death-resurrection involves all of creation which is "waiting to be set free from bondage to decay." This particular moment in history made a real change, and first of all at the subconscious level, at the level at which man is (or can be) in touch with animal and plant life. Recent experiments have shown that plants actually are measurably sensitive to human actions and feelings. If this is so, it can seem less odd to our narrow-minded age that the crisis point of the earth's history, when "death is swallowed up in victory" should affect all living things and our minds at that level, well below the level at which we make conscious acts of faith. It is clear from the Gospel accounts that the risen Jesus had a different and in a sense more "intimate" relationship with material reality than human bodies have in their "deathly" state. In a strange way, this entering of the risen one into a relationship with matter parallels the moment of annunciation and Mary's assent, when the Word and wisdom of God entered into the relationship of incarnation, again a relationship below the conscious level. But this time it is the whole of material reality which "receives" the Word and is transformed by it even without awareness.

There is awareness, the human witnesses supply that and testify to the happening. There has to be this seeing, and touching, and speaking and telling. These "witnesses of the resurrection," then and now, are the makers of the Church, the conscious shapers of a new creation. But what they testify to is an event whose full significance can only be expressed haltingly and in symbols. The deepest and furthest reverberation of this explosion of glory extends into every obscure corner of reality, physical as well as spiritual.

Ever since, Christians have been wrestling with the meaning of it all. Because it is less often considered, it is a help to begin our resurrection, re-think at that strange and near-unconscious level where it changes the visible, touchable world. Nothing can ever be the same again, *we need not be afraid to love.* The things we love will decay and die, but that is not the end. Beauty is fragile, but that is not the end. Growing things may be crushed, ugly factories may cover the fields, chemicals may poison streams and kill the birds and flowers because of man's greed, but that is not the end. We need not harden ourselves to endure, because the endurance has a purpose and a flowering, even within the suffering itself. Death is powerful, and seems victorious, but it is not the end.

There is no Gospel account of the meeting of the risen Jesus with his mother, and many artists and spiritual writers have tried to fill the gap, imagining it for us. But perhaps there was no gap. In her, above all, the awareness below the conscious level must have been acute. The poet Charles Williams, in his poem cycle on the Arthurian legends, sees Galahad, the mysteriously born knight who was pure enough to see the Holy Grail, as a symbol of Christ. He meditates on the woman's vocation, the symbolic stages of her life, her acceptances and her royalty and her motherhood. He is thinking of Mary, and of the virgin Princess Dindrane in the legend, and of all women, and says that:

> "happy the woman who. . . .
> feels Galahad . . . . . rise
> in her flesh, and her flesh bright in Carbonek with Christ,
> in the turn of her body, in the turn of her flesh, in the turn
> of the Heart that heals itself for the healing of others."

It is the flesh, of Mary, and of women and of the feminine, that "feels" him "rise" and that flesh (unconscious, material) is "bright with Christ." In her body, in her flesh, in her heart—or is it *his* heart? Whose is the healed and healing heart? Hers or his? Or both? The poet doesn't say and we can't tell, yet we feel the rightness of the ambiguity. Mary's flesh knows the rising of Christ, as it knew his incarnation. It is possible for women to have this sensitivity, to be aware of resurrection at this level, if they are brave enough.

XII
"At-one-ment"

If our awareness of resurrection can begin at a profound level of sensitive "fleshliness," the upward movement of the ascension completes the transformation. It expresses in visual terms the fact that this fleshly nature, thus brought back into an intimate and new relationship to all of matter, lifts the whole human experience right into the "heavens." Heaven and earth are no longer parted; the gulf of the fall is bridged, indeed annihilated. The human nature whose risen reality affects every molecule in the universe is also the transcendent, the one who transforms by his own power.

You have to know it with your mind, assent to it consciously. The silent awareness of resurrection as a fact of earth and earth's experience is not enough until it makes us *behave* differently. We have to live "as in the light," and to do that we have to be consciously aware of what it's all about. The poem from which I quoted in the last section reflects on this, as the poet meditates on the way in which the physical life of a woman even *un*consciously symbolizes the process of salvation—accepting the seed of new life, bringing it to birth, tending it and feeding it, then giving it up, losing the ability itself to conceive life, and finally accepting death as the completion of the way. One meets women who have achieved an evident wholeness and peace, an inner integrity, simply by fully living their physical womanhood, though they could never explain what it meant. "Flesh knows what spirit knows," says the poet, yet that is not enough. It cannot be a message for others, to break through ignorance, to show the way, unless there is a way to explain. The Spirit must be *conscious.* It must be a spiritual consciousness, yet of the flesh. There must no longer be a separation. "Flesh knows what spirit knows, but spirit *knows* it *knows*," says the poet, and later on repeats it in a slightly different form:

> "Flesh tells what spirit tells
> (but spirit knows it tells). Woman's travel
> holds in the natural the image of the supernatural. . . ."

To know that image and live it is the work of the risen, transformed Self. Even now we can experience this, in privileged, great moments of life and in smaller ones too. There can come a moment of sudden exultation, for no apparent reason. It may be a spring morning, or a baby's unexpected smile, or one of those moments between lovers when there is a sense of oneness so total as to leave no room even for thought. It can happen pegging out the wash, or looking up from a book, or playing a game with a child, or digging the garden. It descends on you, a spasm of intense joy, so that you scarcely dare to move in case it vanishes. Yet it is painful in its perfection, so that it is almost a relief when—very soon, normally—it does vanish.

Such moments can come to anyone, unless their lives are so concentrated on selfish and trivial ends that there is no room for them. But in most lives they leave little trace. They are real, but they have no meaning. Whether they transform a whole life, or leave no trace but a fading nostalgia, depends on how one recognizes them, what one understands about the event. "Flesh knows what spirit knows," so the descent of such an experience of spiritual joy is perfectly genuine in a person with no conscious understanding of the event. But if it is to *work*, it must be not an isolated experience but an upward step toward the spiritual and eternal reality of which it is a foretaste. It has to be a revelation of the existence of such an eternal reality, so that one's life may be directed toward it, consciously, even when the experience itself is only a memory. But for this re-direction there has to be an understanding of what has happened, a *spiritual* understanding, because this is about the transformation of a human being in the spirit. "Spirit *knows* it knows" and can make decisions in the light of that knowledge.

The risen Christ was restored to his friends in a way that challenged them to realize the nature of what had happened, but at first they couldn't. They *experienced* his presence, but they passed from one meeting to the next in a kind of dazed joy, puzzled, wondering, happy, and not yet thinking about the future at all. They simply "absorbed" his presence and his love as much as they could. Later, they remembered words and actions, and reflected on their meaning, and tried to express it, but at the time they knew he was present yet didn't know they knew it. In the walk of the two disciples to Emmaus we see this clearly, for they only "recognized" their companion on the walk at the moment when he broke bread with them—and vanished. And it was the evangelist's hindsight which emphasized that eucharistic gesture as the one which made them know what they knew. But even on the occasions when they knew who it was who was eating or talking with them, the presence of the Lord demanded no more of them than to be there, to know his presence and love. For this moment of new life to become a *way* of life, leading to total transformation, something else had to happen.

That something was the taking away of one kind of experience, precisely so that they might realize its nature and, later, *do* something about it. They had to *know*, but then to *know* that they *knew*. It was not enough to experience that silent, unconscious transformation of the material creation; the human response had also to be a conscious one. And that consciousness reached "up to heaven," for (once it was clear what was actually happening) "heaven" was clearly what it was all about. Heaven was no longer a far-off abode of the ineffable Yahweh, clothed in blinding glory so that man might not approach him. On the contrary, human nature was so profoundly affected in the person of the risen Jesus that it could "reach to heaven," aware of the divine life at the very heart of earthly existence and changing it radically.

The impression given by St. Luke's two accounts of what happened after the ascension of Christ is not at all of a sense of "let-down" or anticlimax, as one might expect. He says the disciples went home "with great joy" and that they "gave themselves to prayer" in the temple and in the home. It all sounds very orderly and deliberate and purposeful, whereas in the period of the "resurrection appearances" there is a sense almost of aimlessness, or at least of merely passive waiting. That is just what we discover if we begin to know the meaning of God's work in us. The moment of inward, unspeakable knowledge gives no scope for reflection, but when it has gone, then is the time for conscious and careful—and prayerful—thought. But not for rushing into action. There has to be a time of assimilation, of discovery, a time for realizing what it's all about, and then turning consciously to God, who will let us know in due course what has to be done.

The line of the design of salvation describes a curve, the curve of transformation, echoing the curve of incarnation. There is a downward curve, an entering into matter, an "at-one-ment," an intimate sharing of unconscious being; then there is a sharp upward curve, a breaking into consciousness, and that consciousness is one sensitive to the presence of the Spirit, Emmanuel, the divine indwelling. Yet the second, transforming curve is bolder and more splendid; it delves deeper and rises higher. It expresses a great embrace, as earth reaches to heaven, and heaven, in more-than-response, breaks open to envelop the human thing within itself and change it, yet making it for the first time fully itself. The last curve includes and perfects the first; the first finds its own meaning explained in the second.

XIII
Flames of the Spirit

We saw the line of transformation echoing the line of incarnation, perfecting and explaining it, but neither completes the design, because it isn't finished. The coming of the Word into the human world had to be known and seen and touched, as St. John says, in the adult public life of Jesus, otherwise it would have remained without effect in the everyday world. In a sense, the mystery has to "come down to earth," be expressed and discussed and used—and misused. So also the triumphant upward flight of ascension does not end in the heavens, it has to "come down to earth," because that is where all the people are who have to be told that they, too, are "heirs of God, co-heirs with Christ." They don't easily believe it, being too busy worrying about inheriting the kingdom of this world. All kinds of extravagant and outrageous (as well as ordinary, patient and plodding) methods are needed to reach all those millions who know (because they *are* human and have Christ "in their flesh" whether they like it or not) but don't "know they know."

The line of transformation continues, then, but it ceases to be a single line. It's like what happens when a rocket goes up—the line of fiery light soars up and up, and everyone watches as it rises, so high it seems it will never stop. Then there is a breathless pause, "a moment in and out of time" when it seems that nothing is happening, and yet the nothing is filled to the brim with expectation. (The time when Mary and the other disciples waited in Jerusalem after the ascension must have had that quality, and so—in a different way—must the years of waiting in Nazareth.) Then, just when the suspense seems ridiculous, the thing happens, there is no longer a soaring line, but the whole sky is suddenly filled with particles of light, and each particle describes its own line, upwards, outwards and downwards. Nobody sees where they end.

We know where they end. They end in the lives of people. Suddenly, or slowly, men and women are enlightened with the huge glory of the Spirit's revelation. But it isn't vast and blinding, nor do they even realize, at first, that it is a shared thing. It is a light for each one, a flame that "sits upon each of them," illuminating his or her little world, revealing it in a new way. This is the extraordinary thing about the working of God in human life. The design of salvation is vaster and more crushingly beautiful than the milky way on a clear night, yet it is as intimate, homely and personal as a bedroom candle.

Most people don't have those nowadays, though when there was a power cut you may have wished you had. I have a bedroom candle, because we have no electricity here, and if we ever do I hope I shall remember my candle. For it is a lovely thing. Its brave little flame is so fragile, so easily blown out, yet if you put a candle on the windowsill your friends can see it a mile or more away. It casts huge shadows, and the room seems full of strange, unexplained shapes and movements which one can forget in daylight. But it is a lovely light, softening faces with a sort of gentle glory. It creates intimacy. No wonder painters like de la Tour loved to paint scenes lit by a single candle, for it creates a unity, it hides away irrelevant day-lit details, leaving only the human faces and figures together in the golden light. A candle will kindle an evening's talk, the kind of talk that can be very deep, and end in a silence which is not negative but full of things unsaid yet understood. And it can light the page of a book for one person to read—or to write. (Interesting to think that much of the world's great literature was written by candlelight.)

It really seems unnecessarily heavy-handed to interpret the symbol too carefully. Christ came to "cast fire on the earth" and it is a fire that transforms the world, yet to each man or woman it is personal and particular and private. It helps us to recognize the indwelling Spirit in other people, but only because we ourselves, our personal secret selves, have this light to keep, it belongs to us as long as we don't blow it out.

The resurrection means the world is changed from inside itself. It "feels" different, to those who know, are sensitive to it, and it looks and is different, to those who "know they know." It makes different demands on them. And if the upward curve of ascension symbolizes this rising to self-consciousness of the act of salvation, it is the coming of the Spirit which symbolizes how the knowledge becomes available to every conscious mind. In the rising and ascension of Jesus the whole process happens, is perfected and shown, but at Pentecost it is proclaimed, the message is made available to limited, fallible human beings and in human words and actions. The message is entrusted to messengers. The Word is to be spoken in words.

And here we come up against one of those moments of slightly unnerving recognition. "But of course—," yet a moment before one hadn't realized. The "of course" is the way it all begins again. The fall of fire-particles from heaven, the candle-flame, the messenger, the spoken word—whatever image you find helpful, what actually happens is this: something new, yet familiar, something strange and frightening yet glorious, comes into the mind of a person. It is a kind of demand, a request for a hearing, it can be refused. Once heard, it can be rejected. But if the message is heard, and the demand accepted (in the tiniest, most insignificant way) then a process is set in motion once more, as it once was in Nazareth. There is incarnation, the Word of God is heard, accepted, and it grows, and is born, and shared; it agonizes and is abused and dies; it transforms, and breaks forth, and is a shower of fire particles over the earth, and each one comes to another innocent, waiting ear.

We are all the angel Gabriel. We are all Mary, virgin and mother; we are all Elizabeth, and Joseph, and Simeon; we all listen to the boy in the Temple, and also seek him sorrowing. We lie on our faces in Gethsemane, we are beaten and mocked, and we beat and mock. We inflict the crown—and wear it, if we may, unknowing. We carry the cross, and help the cross-bearer, and sometimes refuse to, or misunderstand the whole affair; we die on the cross, as best we can, and often nail others to it; we support the dying Christ, or turn away from him.

Christ rises in us, and we in him. We meet him in the garden, or scarcely believe in him, or refuse to; we realize his rising, and ascend to heaven at his side, and watch him rise, and go back to Jerusalem "rejoicing"; we receive the Spirit, and we are the flames of the Spirit, and cast fire on the earth, and proclaim the message, and somebody hears—.

XIV
Instrument of the Harvest

The last two mysteries of the rosary, neither of them found in Scripture, often appear to be merely tacked onto the rest, to round off the story and show reverence for Mary's unique role in the story of salvation. But they are much more than that. At this period of history they have an extraordinary and radical message, and while they complete the story chronologically they also reveal aspects of the whole plan of salvation which we could learn in no other way.

It is important for Catholics to realize this. There is no doubt that reverence and love for Mary have, at times in Catholic history, been distorted and wrongly developed, and so it is understandable that other churches have regarded devotion to Mary with suspicion. It is understandable but it has been disastrous. The loss of the sense of the role of feminine in God's work has allowed the development, almost unhindered, of an emphasis on activity, work, material achievement, as a measure of a person's worth. This has become known, not without reason, as the "Protestant work ethic." It has produced wonders of material progress, accompanied (at first unnoticed) by an increasing loss of spiritual balance, and gradually the whole process has begun to lose self-confidence. It questions its own meaning with growing despair, or tries to hide the questions with more and more activity, further and more grandiose goals to aim at.

At the same time, indeed as part of the same process, there has been an increasing separation of the spiritual from the material. "Situation ethics" are one aspect of this—the idea that it doesn't matter what you do, if you are sincere and "loving" when you do it. The body can act as it will, if only the heart is right. It is the old Manichaean heresy—and it is false and horrible, because the acts of the body are not independent of heart and mind and spirit. The evil in the spirit makes bodily acts evil, yes—but evil of the body (even done in all "sincerity") corrupts the mind and heart. We all realize that this is true when we think about what happens to children brought up in violence and fear. The way they are taught to *behave* makes them the kind of people they become. Yet, in spite of this, we have learned to believe, very easily, that bodily, material acts are unable to affect the spirit. One can make money ruthlessly, for instance, and yet "be a good Christian." Or can one?

The dogma of the assumption of Mary undercuts all this nonsense. The loveliness of Mary is all one, body and mind and spirit. If she is all beautiful spiritually, then her physical body is affected by the fact. Uncorrupted spiritually, to a unique degree, she must be uncorrupted physically. Human beings are one, body-spirit, and are converted and saved as such. Salvation does not consist in the discarding of an evil body by the purified soul, but in the transformation of both. Mary's death marked for her the moment of the completion of that transformation, because there was nothing to prevent it, no residues of ignorance, fear, deceit, defensive attitudes, suspicion, or pride to clog the body's perfect response to the work of the spirit of the risen Christ.

At harvest time, the first stalk of wheat used to be brought in early, to be ground and made into a harvest loaf, used to celebrate the bounty of the fields. It was a symbol of gratitude, confidence, and hope. The rest was still in the fields, where the whole work-force was out laboring under the hot sun to get the harvest in while the weather remained fine. But the harvest loaf was a sign that the thing could be done. Mary is our harvest loaf, the first of the crop. She didn't plant the crop or make it grow, yet without her, the woman, it could not grow. Without the power of the feminine in human beings of both sexes, to accept and to nurture and to offer, salvation could not happen.

The assumption of Mary is, in a sense, the "inside" of the resurrection and ascension of Christ. The Church, his body, enlivened by his spirit, "grows" him, until the harvest, as Mary did. But she is not just the instrument; Mary is "part of" Jesus; the feminine side of human nature "grows" the spirit-in-the-body, until the harvest. Christ, the "first fruit," rises and transforms, but that in him which is feminine, which receives and nurtures and heals and tends, is symbolized by the assumption of Mary—body and soul, one perfect response to God's Word spoken, planted, in her.

So Mary's assumption is not a pious afterthought, or even a special personal reward. It is the essential symbol of redemption; it shows us what it's all about. The human body, a material thing, conditioned by its physical environment, is "the means of grace and the hope of glory." It is the sacrament of God's presence, by which God reaches and makes us, and by which all the seven traditional sacraments have meaning and power. The human body is capable of every kind of abomination, both inflicted and suffered, but still, if it hears the Word, it is capable of glory. We need this mystery of Mary to assure us of that. In a sense, the resurrection of Jesus should tell us all we need to know, but history has shown that Christians are quite capable of living with that great knowledge and yet regarding it as, practically speaking, irrelevant. They could adore the risen Christ, and think of his rising as mainly a proof of his own divinity, nothing to do with us ordinary people (at least not until the last judgment).

Perhaps we don't really *want* to realize the meaning of resurrection. It makes such huge demands on us. To "die with Christ and live with him" seems like too much to cope with. Perhaps that is one reason why many people (not only Protestants) were angry when Pope Pius XII defined the dogma of the assumption of Mary as "of faith." Many said it distracted attention from the unique glory of Jesus and also increased the division between Catholics and Protestants.

Only a very superficial view could assume such things. The realization that Mary's humanness could be so perfected made clear just what the resurrection of Christ had achieved and could achieve. It made it impossible for a thoughtful believer to maintain the fatal separation between body and spirit. Nobody, at the time of the definition, objected to the idea that Mary's *soul* was with God; it was her body they couldn't take. We all have this puritan suspicion of the body tucked away somewhere. The definition of the assumption dragged it out, denied its Christian validity, and left us to wrestle with the moral consequences.

As for the division between Catholics and Protestants, the result has been very interesting—even rather funny! Since that time, many Catholics have been re-thinking devotion to Mary, and some seemed to lose it altogether, at least for a time. They are gradually recovering it, in many ways, enhanced by the need for re-discovery. But meanwhile many Protestants, unhampered by previous mistakes as Catholics were, have been discovering Mary for the first time. They have been discovering the dimension of spirituality which she symbolizes, and their religious understanding has grown in depth and balance accordingly. (The most successful recent book on the rosary was written by a Methodist.)

This is not accidental. There is a terrible thirst, in our overconscious, mechanized, frenetic and frightened culture, for the sense of stability, reflection, enduring courage and healing which is signified by the role of Mary. She means, for us, the tenderness and yet toughness of God's handling of us, as a mother has to be tender and tough to raise her family properly. But she also means that all this is caught up to heaven itself. We call God Father, "Father," that is Life-giver, but in Scripture God is also Mother. In the dogma of the assumption we see the feminine aspects of God-in-man fully acknowledged, venerated, raised to the heights of heaven. Forevermore, the sign of final glory has a woman at the heart of it, "clothed with the sun, and on her head a crown of twelve stars."

XV
The Queen of Heaven

The assumption and coronation of Mary, like the resurrection and ascension of Jesus, are one movement, symbolized in two different ways. I have tried to indicate (and you can't imagine how hard it is to put this into words, until you've tried) what I called a "design," the "curve" of God's work of salvation. I discovered two "curves," following each other roughly in outline, the line of incarnation and the line of transformation, yet the first really only makes sense in relation to the second. But here, in these last two mysteries, the metaphor of a "curve" is inadequate, because in a sense the shape is the same, the rising and glory, one upward movement. The relationship is very close—so close that there is really only one movement, but the upward sweep of Mary's glorification is part of the "inwardness" of the rising curve of the victorious Christ.

Perhaps it is easier to think of the relationship in terms of music. The theme of incarnation is stated, and developed, then the theme of death—different, discordant, harsh, yet harmonically related—takes the theme to bits and makes our ears almost "forget" the first one. But the first then returns, only this time it is changed, it is more sweeping and compelling, rising to a triumphant climax. But as it develops there is heard a version of the main theme, like it and yet not the same, developing in a way that brings out aspects that the main statement could not include. This secondary yet essential theme runs "under" the first and final one, crossing the rhythm of it and reinforcing it, adding a dimension of meaning that completes the whole, so that both come together in the final concord.

That is as near as I can get to expressing the relationship that I perceive. The raising of Mary to be "Queen of Heaven" is a symbolic statement that fittingly closes the cycle of fifteen, but it has an especial significance for the understanding of womanhood, and the feminine aspect of life, in our time. To the Protestant psychologist Jung, the definition of the assumption was "the most important religious event for four hundred years," because it marked a movement in history when human beings were able to bring the feminine *to full consciousness* and realize it as *spiritual.* This may seem obvious, but the fact is that for most of human history the feminine aspect of life has been identified with the unconscious, dark, material aspects of life. The old mother-goddesses and virgin-goddesses were symbols of earth, of fertility, or of uncontrolled passion, of the strange gifts of magic and soothsaying, and also of night, death and the underworld generally. The feminine, then, is seen as apt to be evil; it is certainly dangerous to orderly consciousness and social relationships. It must be kept "under," symbolically, or it might destroy human life. It is not surprising that it was feared and suppressed, in the persons of women, and in the *minds* of women themselves. The final reaction to this, in many women, has been to disown the feminine and assert the masculine in themselves in order to re-claim a proper place in a masculine type of culture. Thus they re-inforced the already unbalanced character of our society, at a time when, to quote Jung, "the achievements of science and technology, combined with a rationalistic and materialistic view of the world, threaten the spiritual and psychic heritage of man with instant annihilation." He was talking about "the bomb," but only as a symptom (no doubt the final one) of a very sick society.

And what happened? Something happened—something had been building up—in the feminine consciousness. For a long time it was only half aware, a restlessness and discontent without clear goals. Then it found a partial goal—political status, the vote. That was symbolic of the desire to be "persons"; in itself, of course, it wasn't enough. "Women's Lib." erupted, searching and demanding, not always clear or realistic, often angry and destructive. That destructiveness was the old, dark, powerful "earth mother" getting her revenge for neglect, and it showed where the mistake lay. The problem for women was how to discover and take on a full and equal role in society, how to be fully persons, without being pseudo men, or becoming vengeful furies. The Eumenides—the Furies—were the terrible females sent by the gods to avenge crimes against the social order and peace. They have been loosed on our society, for its crimes against human life and relationships, and justly loosed. But to be an instrument of divine vengeance is not a very happy role for a woman's lifetime.

In the middle of all this, at a time when the

feminine self-awareness was still struggling to discover itself, to have a meaning, there occurred the definition of Mary's assumption. Jung saw this event as the assertion that the dark earth mother is no longer dark, is in fact "enthroned in heaven," yet she is still the earth, still the place where life develops. This was certainly *not* uppermost in the mind of Pope Pius and those who advised him. But, symbolically, this was what the declaration "said." That is the nature of symbols, they are not arbitrary, they are not invented, they belong to the nature of an event or personal role, everyone *feels* their power, even if they have no idea of their significance.

A crown, as we saw earlier, is a symbol. The coronation of Mary is God's assertion of the divine royalty of the feminine role in salvation. What does it mean for ordinary women, searching for a sense of hope and identity in a time when roles are fluid and society unsure of its goals?

I think it means something absolutely solid and basic. It means that I, as a woman, have in me the divine power in a particular way. (It is in men and women both, but men have to use the feminine in themselves in a different way.) The power that once was feared and despised because it was intuitive, connected with the unconscious, linking man to earth and to animal life, can now be *loved* and *revered* for the same reasons. For there is no need to escape the earth and the unconscious and the kinship with other kinds of life, rather there is the need to transform them. When I know they *can* be transformed, because they *have* been, then I need not fear them, or fear to be kept by them in a state of suppression. Instead of having to reject the feminine in order to be a person, I can recognize it, crowned and glorified, in the heart of God. So the great Dante saw it, at the heart of the Trinity, when Beatrice, the woman who leads to God, showed him this final revelation.

It is really impossible to draw an exact line between aspects of personality which are masculine and those which are feminine, because the differences depend a good deal on the kind of society you live in. A lot of it has to go by "feel" too. And there is this to consider—if *women* can learn to value and "glorify" their feminine qualities, then *men* will learn to recognize the feminine in themselves without being ashamed or afraid of it, and therefore they won't feel the need to keep bashing it in the persons of women. So it matters to have a reasonably clear idea of what one means by feminine qualities. (I repeat that it is necessary to recognize, appreciate and develop your masculine ones, too, but that is not what we are considering now.)

One way we can try to gain an insight into the feminine role is to think about royalty—the royalty of Mary, crowned Queen of Heaven. We think of a king as the one who rules by right, making laws and enforcing them, creating the structures of society, defending his people, planning for their safety and prosperity. But we think of a queen as ruling by choice—the king's choice and her own. Her rule is of a different kind, for she shapes the laws to the needs of the people, she creates within the framework of law a way of life for her people, in which each has room to grow. She is the healer, the reconciler, the peacemaker. When there were kings and queens who really ruled, of course these roles were combined and swapped around, according to differing personalities, because people aren't *just* symbols. But they *are* symbols, all the same. The symbol of the queen is a very powerful one, and vital to the future of ourselves and our world, at a time when the idea of authority is almost entirely "Kingly" even at its best.

Mary, the Queen of Heaven, is the symbol of the role of queenship in every woman. In every woman, then, she is present, for a symbol *works*. In each there is a call to the vocation of queenship, a call to the dedication of the ruler who is mother in generosity, virgin in single-hearted commitment. She is healer and peacemaker, reconciling in herself the warring symbols that set men and women against each other, children against parents and parents against children. She is terrible, too, "like an army with banners," because the sign of the woman in heaven is a sign of doom for the powers of darkness that thrive on servility and hypocrisy and emotional blackmail—the weapons of women who have never learned to see the crown of twelve stars.

Every time I say the rosary I realize afresh how much I have to learn. But I realize that even by holding these great symbolic mysteries in my mind for a little while, I am giving the symbols a chance to grow. It doesn't matter if we can't *think* about them. They work by their own power, just by being brought into consciousness for a time, in a confused way. There is no need to draw conscious lessons from them. They are Words of God, they have their own life and power. And part of their power lies in the fact that they are Mary's symbols, never separable from the whole design of God, but hers because they grew, and grow, in the woman, take life from her, and give her life. She is the sign in all these signs, a sign for our time and for ourselves, "a great sign in heaven."